TH
COFFEE
AT WOODFORD

LIFE IN WOODFORD GREEN, 1890–1920

WITH AN APPENDIX ON THE COFFEE HOUSE
MOVEMENT IN THE UK

BY

EVE LOCKINGTON
AND
WIN TRICKEY

LOUGHTON
THE LOUGHTON AND DISTRICT HISTORICAL SOCIETY
2002

© Eve Lockington and Win Trickey 2002

ISBN
0954 2314 14

First published in 2002 by the
Loughton and District Historical Society
and available from Forest Villa, Staples Road
Loughton, Essex
IG10 1HP

Cover design and plates by
Artform
Little Tew OX7 4JH

Printed in Great Britain by
The Headway Press Ltd
Reading

Contents

Illustrations

Foreword

The Coffee House from which this book takes its title was built across the parish boundary of Walthamstow and Woodford, which runs some 100 yards to the west of Woodford High Road. Its occupiers paid rates to both boroughs. But why, it might be asked, should the Loughton and District Historical Society publish a book about a café situated some two miles from the boundary of its own area?

The answer to this is threefold. First, Eve Lockington, who wrote the book, basing it on research done by her sister, Win Trickey, is the LDHS's treasurer. Secondly, those members of the committee who read the manuscript were immediately convinced that here was a real gem of local history, and one that put human flesh on the bones of local fact. Thirdly, the temperance movement was strong throughout south-west Essex, marching in the late nineteenth century for the most part with nonconformity. So although the book deals with the Ensom family, its story might be repeated in many of the temperance establishments of the Forest area, the Retreats, the tea gardens, the 'teapot rows' of Forest Road and Smarts Lane in Loughton, up to the great Wilfrid Lawson Temperance Hotel which was sited no more than five minutes' walk from the Coffee House.

As the account reveals, the Ensom family were practising Congregationalists. The Coffee House was situated right in front of what had been Woodford's first nonconformist church, the Mill Lane Chapel, established in 1794. Whether the ground once belonged to the chapel we do not know, but it is tempting to speculate so. The family story was that the building was once a school, with a single large room suitable for teaching. We know that the nonconformist British School was carried on in Mill Lane Chapel, but the numbers of children educated there in the 1850s and 60s would hardly have fitted into the small chapel building. Perhaps the Coffee House was built on or next to the chapel ground as the boys' or girls' accommodation?

After the 1870 Education Act, the British School was closed and the children sent instead to the enlarged National School which became the Green School of this narrative. The worshippers of Mill Lane Chapel had also moved, first to the Providence Chapel at the top of Horn Lane, and then into the magnificent 1870s church on that site, with its great Gothic spire, sadly demolished after a direct hit in 1944 by a flying bomb.

Methodists of various denominations later used the little chapel. Then it became a mission hall in Woodford of the Pleasant Sunday Afternoon movement, which in Loughton flourished in the Lincoln Hall opposite the Union Church.

In any case, at the time of the Ensoms, the owner of the café was Ebenezer Clarke, Jr, of Walthamstow, described by the late Tony Law in his preface to Clarke's own *Walthamstow Past, Present and Future* (1861, facsimile reprint, 1981) as a noted nonconformist philanthropist. The Coffee House was most likely a practical way of supporting the temperance cause by keeping the locals and passing carmen (carters) out of the pubs, of which there were three within a minute's walk.

Jack Farmer, in his *Woodford as I Knew It*, says:

'Down Mill Lane, The Square and Castle Yard was a little community, with their own grocer, greengrocer, boot repairer, watchmaker . . . The old coffee shop . . . had been run for years by Mrs Ensom, and was carried on by her daughter, Mrs Collins after she retired . . . Mrs Collins was greatly respected and loved. The premises stood half in Woodford and half in Walthamstow.'

The human interest of this story is immense. A typical late Victorian working class family of six children, in accommodation that would suit two at the most; an autocratic father; every last halfpenny precious; the educational system that despite 60 in a class and poorly trained teachers, turned out people competent in basic skills – all these are covered. The vignette of life on the edge of London and the border of the forest would have been repeated all over the area, but what gives this account its special merit is that it is told, through family memories, photographs and letters, in the mouths of actual people. If one superimposes the vivid account given by this book on the contemporary notes of William Waller for Loughton (*Loughton a Hundred Years Ago*, LDHS, 2001) and the drawings of Octavius Dixie Deacon (in the Epping Forest District Museum), then a real insight into life in the Forest suburbs at the end of the nineteenth century emerges. The local historian can aim at no higher task.

CHRIS POND
Chairman LDHS   February 2002

Preface

This is a story not about big houses, of which at the time there were still a great many in Woodford, nor about approaching urban development from London, which was taking place in South Woodford, but about one family that lived at the back of the Castle in Woodford Green, and about the day-to-day events in the community at the end of the nineteenth century.

It is a story based on research into copies of old newspapers, and also on family stories and anecdotes told to us mainly by our mother – Daisy – and her sister, Rhoda. Chapter 9 is however based on a written record prepared by our father, Richard, in the 1920s.

What was remembered by one member of the family is not always substantiated by another. Obviously some of what is written must be conjectural, but it is an honest attempt to portray the life of a family, not poverty-stricken by any means, but often having a struggle to maintain a satisfactory standard of life. It is a family where the father appears to have been a rather unpleasant autocrat, but where the mother sought the happiness and advancement of her children.

EL
WT   February 2002

DAISY'S FAMILY TREE
as mentioned in the text

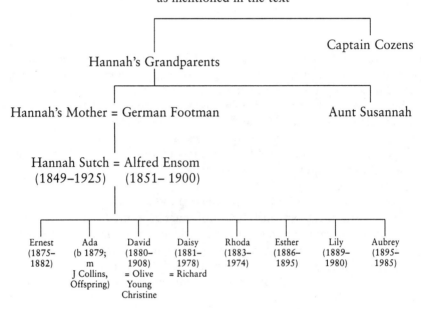

Hannah's Grandparents — Captain Cozens

Hannah's Mother = German Footman — Aunt Susannah

Hannah Sutch = Alfred Ensom
(1849–1925)   (1851– 1900)

| Ernest (1875–1882) | Ada (b 1879; m J Collins, Offspring) | David (1880–1908) = Olive Young Christine | Daisy (1881–1978) = Richard | Rhoda (1883–1974) | Esther (1886–1895) | Lily (1889–1980) | Aubrey (1895–1985) |

1

The Coffee House

The home was a somewhat unusual one. Set in a square, with a large tenement block behind and small cottages alongside, it stood sturdily facing the west. The building had the impressive name of the George and Dragon Coaching House, but to everyone around it was simply 'The Coffee House', though very little coffee was in fact served there.

This so called 'coffee house' was the home of Daisy and her brothers and sisters and was situated in the, then, village of Woodford Green, nine miles from London on the edge of Epping Forest.

When Daisy and her siblings were young, towards the end of the nineteenth century, a good deal of horse-drawn traffic used to pass through the village on the way north and, other than the public-houses, there were very few places where van men could obtain reasonably priced food.

It was a time when there was a great deal of drunkenness and much misery was caused to the poorer members of the community by the breadwinner spending his meagre earnings in the pub in an endeavour to forget the drabness of his existence. When he finally returned home, probably quarrelsome, there would be little money left for the necessities of the family.

Certain wealthy people in the local community had decided there should be a place other than a public-house where workmen could eat at reasonable prices and enjoy a warm room and perhaps a game of dominoes, draughts or chess. They had chosen the building in The Square and called it 'The George and Dragon'; a local artist painted a sign to hang outside. However Alfred, the children's father, did not like the sign and it disappeared.

The building was composed of one large room downstairs which was furnished with long tables and benches. At the end of this room was a door leading to stairs which climbed up to a bedroom and a parlour, the latter turning into a bedroom as the family grew in size. At the other end of the large room a door led into the kitchen, which was the work room and living room of the family. Its main feature was a large black range on which all the cooking for the customers and family was done. This range made the kitchen warm and comfortable in the winter but the room became unbearably hot in the summer when their private door to The Square had to be left open. A dark scullery with a large sink and a cold water tap led off from the kitchen and beyond that was an even darker spider-ridden lavatory. Underneath all was a black storage cellar.

Daisy was the second girl in the family. Her eldest sister, Ada, went early

1

into service, so Daisy became her mother Hannah's much needed help. There had originally been seven children but the eldest son, Ernest, had died at the age of four and, after Ada had gone into service, five other children, David, Daisy, Rhoda, Esther and Lily, were still left at home. The father was disappointed that so many of his children were girls – he had wanted sons to his name. Seven years after the birth of Lily he did, in fact, have another son, Aubrey, who became his darling .

When Daisy's parents first moved into the Coffee House in the mid-1880s the drains had been defective and Ernest, the first born, was said to have caught diphtheria from them and died. Although the drains had been repaired and none of the other children caught this dreaded disease, the house was rather damp and the children suffered from rheumatism.

Why or how her parents had been chosen to run the Coffee House, when Hannah had been taught fine needlework and Alfred had been a carpenter, Daisy never knew. However, many years later it came to light that, while Hannah was in service in a big house in the area, she became pregnant by Alfred. Her employers (who are presumed to have been the Spicer family because that family took such a continuing interest in Hannah's family), thought so much of Hannah that they set the couple up in the Coffee House on their marriage.

Their choice, however, had been a good one. Hannah was clearly a woman of much ability and, although a rather unpleasant father, Alfred had a pleasant manner with the customers and was fairly popular.

Daisy's grandparents had been in service. Her grandfather, a German, was a footman in the house where her grandmother was a housemaid and a very attractive one too. The young housemaid succumbed to the charms of the German footman, which resulted in an unfortunate pregnancy.

Hannah was brought up by her grandparents. No suggestion was made by any member of the family that Hannah might have been illegitimate and yet that probably was the case. Hannah was given her father's surname, 'Sutch'. She very rarely saw her mother who, in time, obtained the position of housekeeper in a large house, quite an important post in those times and one which she could not have obtained if she had been encumbered with a young child. However, she must have regretted her affair with the attractive footman. Her cousin, Edward Cozens, had wanted to marry her, but she turned him down. However Edward went to sea and his father paid for him to be taught navigation. On one voyage he brought the ship safely back to port after the captain had fallen ill. Subsequently he became a captain himself and relatively wealthy. He never married Hannah's mother but took an interest in Hannah and in Hannah's children. Many years later, after he and his wife had died, his money came to Daisy and her brothers and sisters. Divided amongst so many, no one got a vast amount, but Daisy's share was to prove of great assistance later during the difficult times of the 1930s.

Hannah was brought up in London in a tenement block by her grandparents, with assistance from her aunt Susannah. She had a happy childhood and was much loved. Her grandfather who was a bookbinder, was one of the original employees of the stationery firm, W H Smith. As the oldest original employee he had held in his arms the grandson of the founder of the firm. Hannah's grandfather had hoped to have his granddaughter trained as a schoolteacher but then became afraid that he might not live until her training was completed. Instead she was taught fine needlework and dressmaking. She became extremely good at this, so much so that clients would take her to famous fashion houses and point out the dresses they liked. Hannah would then go home and make a copy at a fraction of the cost of the original. Unfortunately this fine work was very bad for her eyes and her sight deteriorated.

Whilst living in London she became very friendly with a young man who lived in the same tenement block. Now secretly Hannah liked him very much indeed and perhaps hoped to marry him. One day he proposed to her, and, though she was very pleased, she was a flirtatious young lady and lightly turned down the offer. If indeed she had wished to marry him, and many years later Daisy believed this was the case, she was very foolish indeed. The young man was a Quaker to whom a nay was a nay and a yea a yea, and he never asked her again.

Subsequently Hannah met Alfred Ensom, a carpenter, who was very good looking, and married him. None of the children knew how their parents had met and their father was feared and disliked by them all. He was the absolute ruler of the household, the owner of his wife and children. His children disliked him so much that they never wished to know anything about his childhood. Although at times they did meet their cousins, after Alfred had died at the age of 49, there was no further contact with them.

Alfred, when young, had rheumatic fever, which damaged his heart, and this may have been the reason why he gave up his trade. He was a very capable man and when the family grew too large for the accommodation at the Coffee House, he floored over the loft and put in a small window. One end of this loft was used as storage space, the other as a bedroom for the girls, who used to have to climb a ladder to their loft bedroom. As they scrambled up they were afraid that someone or something terrible would clutch at their feet and send them crashing down to their deaths. The loft was dark and eerie at all times of the year but especially so in winter. No gas-light brightened the gloom, although the rest of the house was lighted by this means. On dark nights, by the dim light filtering through the opening, the girls would find and light their candles and by the flickering flames get ready for bed. Once in bed they would leave them alight a while and watch the shadows dance on the walls when a breeze caught the flames, until their mother called 'Good night' and the candles had to be extinguished.

The building was taller than the surrounding cottages and on summer evenings, through the little window, the girls had a good view of the village and surrounding countryside. However when the wind howled round the four sides and tugged at the chimney the girls would shudder with fear feeling the building sway and expecting it to crash to the square below. One hundred years later the building is still standing.

Hannah's pretty mother had a sister named Susannah, a plain dumpy woman, whose pleasant personality made up for her lack of good looks. She was loved and appreciated by all who knew her. She helped her parents look after her niece, who preferred her aunt Susannah to her own rather remote mother. Later, all Hannah's children adored their great-aunt and looked forward to her visits.

Susannah had hoped that Daisy would be named after her, but Hannah, though she loved her aunt, did not like her name. Daisy didn't like it either and was extremely grateful to her mother for insisting that it should be her third name.

At the time the children knew their great-aunt, she was living in a tiny almshouse in Clapham. It had one room upstairs, one room downstairs and a very small kitchen.

Having no grandchildren of her own, she adopted Hannah's family and could always be called on for help. She bought a Singer sewing machine in 1875, with which she was able to do much needed needlework for her niece. There were sheets to mend and new ones to make. Hannah's sheeting was always bought by the length. There were clothes to make for the children and although Hannah was a wonderful manager, keeping her growing family clothed would have been very difficult without the loving help given her by her aunt.

This sewing machine never failed. Daisy inherited it from her great-aunt and made clothes for her children with it. It was finally sold after the Second World War and then only because of the difficulty in obtaining the right kind of needles for it. The machine was an attractive one, pleasantly decorated with mother-of-pearl. It could be stowed away in a sturdy but attractively made case.

All the children loved their great-aunt Susannah dearly, but undoubtedly she had a favourite, her namesake Daisy Mary-Susannah. Once when Daisy was very young, Susannah asked if the child could come and stay with her for a few days in her tiny almshouse home. Daisy was very excited at the idea; it would be an adventure for her and she looked forward to the visit impatiently. Alas, the visit was not a success, for Daisy soon became very homesick. There were no other children to play with and she wandered around disconsolately. Nothing her aunt could do would interest her. Then she started to cry 'I want David and Rhoda' she sobbed. Susannah tried to pacify the homesick child but to no avail. Then in the night Daisy developed earache and cried again, this time with pain. Poor Susannah! She had so much looked forward to having the child with her. She was worried in case

Daisy became seriously ill and she would not know what to do. So in the morning, very upset at the failure of her experiment, she took the little girl back home. Nevertheless, although Daisy did not wish to stay with her aunt, she loved her aunt to visit them, which she did frequently, especially when the children were young and her niece needed her assistance.

Most of the customers of the Coffee House were van men who used to put nose bags full of corn on their horses, when they tethered them outside the shop. The horses would toss their heads in the air and down would fall some of the grain to the ground.

Alfred noticed this, and being an astute man, bought two dozen chickens which were allowed to run loose around The Square. He fixed nesting boxes to the end of the building and in due course the hens started to lay. In fact they laid very well indeed and Alfred decided that, as the hens had been fed on such good grain, the eggs surely must be the best available, so any surplus to the family's requirements were sold locally and the children had to hawk them round the wealthy houses in the area. Because he considered that the eggs were the best around, they had to be sold at a halfpenny more per dozen than any others. A halfpenny was quite a sum in those days, and the children found it very hard to get customers.

Alfred left the running of the coffee house to Hannah – such work he considered beneath him, but he would stroll through the shop, wander up to some favoured customer and pass the time of day with him. He would also play draughts and chess with the men, being particularly good at the latter game. All the hard work and organisation of the place he left to Hannah.

However, although he did not help with the Coffee House, he did work hard on other projects for the benefit of the family. In 1887, when Bancroft's School was being built at Woodford Wells, he acquired a tea kiosk and installed it in the vicinity. His health at that time was still reasonably good and he would take tea to the workmen, walking skilfully along the scaffolding carrying billycans, while Daisy and her brother David, brought along to help and to get them from under their mother's feet, would watch from below, their mouths hanging open in apprehension. Then in the early autumn when the nights were cool and moist and the blackberries in the forest black and juicy, Alfred would return to the kiosk remaining there all night to supply hot tea and mountains of bread and butter to the blackberry boys. These lads would come from the East End of London equipped with baskets and lanterns and would spend the night quietly combing the forest for blackberries, an arduous, prickly task at the best of times but made doubly arduous and prickly when the only light was that of moving lanterns and the harvest moon.

After a night picking blackberries the boys were only too pleased to refresh themselves at Alfred's kiosk before returning to London in time to catch the early market trade. And Alfred, too, was pleased to add a little more to the family's slender financial resources, resources which had to bear the additional strain of paying for four children at school. At that time children were still being charged twopence each per week. How pleased Hannah and Alfred must have been when, in 1891, free education was introduced for all children up to the age of 14.

When Bancroft's School was completed there was no further need for the kiosk at Woodford Wells, so Alfred stationed it much nearer to London, opposite the Rising Sun public-house in Upper Walthamstow. For some years he ran the tea stall there until one night, after the family had gone to bed, they were awoken by a loud banging on the door. It was a policeman. The stall had attracted the attention of local vandals who had tipped it over and ransacked it. There were, however, no funds available to repair and restock the kiosk, so that source of income was lost, a blow to the financial resources of the family.

Despite increasing ill-health, Daisy's father rented an allotment in another part of Woodford. Again the horses tethered round the shop were useful. The children would be ordered to collect the manure which they piled on to a wheelbarrow which Daisy's brother, David, had to wheel down to the allotment about a mile away. The barrow was extremely heavy with the wheel bound with an iron ring. It was difficult enough wheeling it down to the allotment but at least the journey was downhill. Coming back was another matter because Alfred would load any produce he could find onto the barrow and poor David had to push it back, this time up hill all the way.

Another of Alfred's activities – not for the benefit of the family this time – was winemaking. His parsnip variety was considered particularly good and very potent. This hobby, however, was brought to an abrupt halt. A neighbour called in one day for a chat, just after Alfred had broached a new bottle of his wine. He offered a glass to his friend and it was readily accepted as was a further glass. Perhaps the wine was more potent than usual, or his friend was not used to alcohol but the unfortunate fact remained that the man reeled from the 'temperance' coffee house intoxicated. Alfred was appalled; would they be turned out of their home if the story got around? He realised he was putting the reputation of the Coffee House at risk as well as their livelihood. There seemed only one thing to be done. He opened all his bottles of wine and poured the contents down the drain, which must have had a potent odour for a while.

Why it was called a coffee house is a mystery. Very little coffee was served and that was generally made from essence out of a bottle. Mostly the customers had tea or lemonade. The menu for the day was written on a board outside the shop and usually comprised a cut off a joint, often a bacon joint, or steak and kidney pie, and a pudding. The customers were also able to have two different vegetables with their meat course. Catering for a fluctuating clientele, without a refrigerator, while still holding prices

6

down to a minimum and avoiding wastage, must have been extremely difficult for Hannah.

However, whatever problems Hannah had in running the Coffee House and caring for her brood of children, there was one thing she always insisted on. None of the family must ever go to school, or later work, without a good breakfast, generally eggs boiled or fried. The father insisted on having fried bacon with his eggs and, for a special treat, the children were allowed to wipe round the frying pan with a piece of bread, which soaked up the delicious 'mucky stuff' as they called the bacon fat. No doubt Hannah insisted on a good breakfast for the children because she was always busy in the shop at lunch time, and coming home from school at midday, the children would eat what they could find for themselves, usually bread and cheese or bread and jam.

Hannah was an excellent cook. She made jams, pickles, bottled fruit and baked cakes. Bread was made by the local village baker. She roasted the meat and prepared all the pies and puddings for the shop. Lily, when she was 90 years of age, said she could still see the rows of meat pies keeping warm on the hob, and smell their delicious fragrance. No doubt the children hoped that all the food would not be eaten and that there would be some left for them in the evening.

Hannah had plenty of vegetables from the allotment. These were put into a large pot together with a marrow bone, and cooked for a long time, making nourishing soup which the family would have in the evening. The children loved their mother's steamed puddings. Hannah used to make a plain pudding and the children could choose what to have with it – should it be treacle, jam, or a knob of butter with a spoonful of sugar? Before going to bed the children, if still hungry, could have bread and milk with sugar, or, if they preferred, 'pepper and salt sop'. This was made with bread soaked in hot water with a lump of butter added and sprinkled with salt and pepper. It was quick and simple to make but quite tasty and filling.

The children, of course, liked different things. Daisy always enjoyed fruit and, if ever she got the chance, would steal away to a quiet corner with a favourite book and a purloined apple or orange, and there would forget the everyday world until, once again, it caught up with her.

Rhoda's great delight was her mother's pickles. Hannah's pickles were extremely tasty, made of any fruits and vegetables she could get, either from the allotment or cheaply from local farms or greengrocers. When they were being prepared, the aroma drifted throughout the whole building and, on returning from school, was sniffed delightedly by Rhoda. If no one was looking she would get a spoon and help herself. On one occasion, when no one was around, she opened a jar and took a spoonful of her mother's delicious apple chutney. One spoonful was not enough for the greedy child who took another and then began to cough. Unfortunately she did not heed the warning and had another spoonful. It was one spoonful too many and the child started to choke. She could not get her breath and, turning blue, gasped for air. Fortunately, at that moment, Hannah came into the kitchen and guessed what had happened. Indeed it would have been hard not to with the incriminating jar of chutney on the table. She banged Rhoda's back hard and then shook her violently until the child gradually recovered her breath.

The children rarely had pocket money, such a luxury was not for them. Occasionally, however, they were given, not pennies but farthings for their birthday treats. The day Daisy was nine years old she was given a halfpenny. She had been helping, or hindering, Susannah, make clothes for Lily, then a baby of 12 months or so. All Lily's clothes had been passed on from the other children and were much the worse for wear. As usual Susannah had come to the rescue and, at Hannah's request, was making Lily two new dresses. Daisy was at her aunt's side. In view of the fact that it was her birthday and she had been 'helping', Susannah gave the child a whole halfpenny. This was unimaginable wealth. Daisy looked at it delightedly and ran off to show Rhoda. After getting permission from their mother, the two young girls set out to spend Daisy's wealth. They must not waste it but must get the best value for their money. There were two shops in the village at that time which sold sweets. The children went from one to the other peering in the windows to see what they could buy. They both loved aniseed balls – large and tasty – but would not get many even for a halfpenny. There was no doubt about it, the best buy would be 'chew girls chews'. These were strips of toffee, possibly of inferior quality, about a foot long and cost one farthing, so the sisters would be able to have one each. But wait! Surely the 'chew girls chews' were longer in the other shop. Back and forth between the shops ran the little girls until, at last, they had made up their minds and, of course, exasperated the shopkeepers. In the end, Daisy and Rhoda were satisfied that they had spent the precious coin wisely and returned home, unable to speak, their teeth firmly glued to the toffee.

Apart from Esther, nicknamed Etty, who was chronically ill, the children on the whole kept fairly healthy and, because of the expense of medical treatment, Hannah had her own remedies for the children's ailments, which usually worked quite well. For colds they were always given a bowl of onion gruel, made by cooking onions in milk until they were soft and then seasoning well with salt and pepper. It did not cure colds, of course, but would comfort rough throats sore from coughing. When the children had bad coughs, their chests were rubbed with camphorated oil and then wrapped round with flannel.

The cure for earache was heat. One way of administering this was through a salt bag, which was made of thick double flannel, filled with salt heated in a saucepan. The top of the bag was then tied tightly to stop the salt getting out. A salt bag kept hot for a very long time and could be placed right against the afflicted ear bringing comfort and relief to the sick child. A fig poultice was the remedy for a boil and proved very effective in bringing it to a head.

Rhoda was subject to sore throats which in turn produced very bad earache. The salt bags were in constant use but in the end Hannah had to resort to the doctor. He was horrified at the state of the child's tonsils and said that they must be removed as soon as possible. He did not suggest that she should go into a hospital for this simple operation, he would do it in his surgery. 'Bring the child along at 11 am tomorrow', he ordered. As arranged Alfred took Rhoda to the surgery the next morning. When they entered the room the doctor had his hands behind his back as if hiding something. He walked over to the child, told her to open her mouth wide, then, with the instruments until then kept hidden, he cut out the offending tonsils. There was no question of using an anaesthetic, he just cut them out then and there, after which the little girl was expected to walk home.

Poor Rhoda! The shock and pain was intense and she was crying and spitting out blood. Her father told her not to be a baby, she was a big girl now. But even he had a little sympathy for the suffering child and as they were near the fishmonger's shop, he called in and asked the shopkeeper for a piece of the ice in which the fish was kept cool, for his daughter to suck. The fishmonger looked at Rhoda's white and tear-stained face, 'My, she do look right poorly'. He sorted amongst the fish lying on the counter and produced a piece of ice. 'This looks nice and clean, missy, you suck it, it'll make your throat feel much better.' Rhoda still sobbing quietly, took the ice gratefully and sucked it the rest of the way home. She found that it did alleviate the pain a little and lessened the bleeding. When one considers the care with which children's tonsils are now removed and the very real dangers that can attach to the operation, it was remarkable that Rhoda suffered no ill-effects. In fact the effects were only good. Though the operation had been performed so primitively, yet it was well done. The tonsils were completely removed and never regrew. From that day her health improved and she rarely had sore throats.

It is interesting that about five years later, Lily was also having a great many sore throats and the doctor said that she too must have her tonsils out. But on this occasion there was no question of her walking to the doctor's surgery and having them snipped out without anaesthetic, and then sucking fishmonger's ice as she walked home. By this time the Jubilee Hospital had been built. Lily was admitted, had her tonsils removed under anaesthetic in an operating theatre and was kept in overnight. It was only a relatively short while after Rhoda had been treated in so primitive and callous a manner, yet the difference occasioned by the building of the hospital had made life so much easier for the younger sister. It may also have been that Hannah, having by this time lost Esther, was more concerned for Lily and made sure that the child had the best treatment possible.

When the children were young, Hannah had to have some assistance.

She employed a young girl called Jane. Daisy could remember very little about her, only the bare fact that she came there to help her mother. If Jane 'lived in' it is hard to imagine where she could have slept, perhaps in the kitchen or with the girls. Daisy did not remember. This type of domestic service was certainly the lowest rung of the ladder and yet the girl would have been kindly treated by Hannah and not contemptuously, as was Daisy on her brief incursion into domestic service.

The other form of outside help Hannah had was the assistance of a washerwoman. This woman would come in once a week to do all the family's laundry. In order that she might have plenty of really hot water, a boiler was lit in the scullery the evening before and kept alight all night. Hot water could also be obtained from a tap in front of the range.

With this small amount of additional help and with occasional assistance from Aunt Susannah, Hannah capably ran the home, the Coffee House and cared for the children and a sick and demanding husband, an enormous load under which a lesser woman would have collapsed. The devotion with which her children regarded her showed the extent of her success.

2
The Board School on the Green

In the autumn term of 1894, Hannah decided that Daisy, now aged 13, should remain at school for another year in the hope that, at the end, she would be accepted as a pupil teacher. Had Alfred realised that this was the final intention he would have strenuously opposed any extension of Daisy's schooldays. However Hannah had not discussed the matter with him and, as he was uninterested in the welfare of his daughters, he usually left their concerns in his wife's hands. So merely grumbling 'She ought be earning some money by now, I was at her age', he acquiesced, suspecting it was a way for his wife to keep the girl at home and have her assistance with the younger children.

As long as she could remember, it had been Daisy's ambition to become a teacher. She knew that it had originally been the hope of Hannah's grandfather for his adored grandchild. Daisy's mother, deprived of the chance of achieving this for herself, now hoped that her child could become a schoolteacher. Daisy enjoyed reading and most of the other subjects, but in her busy crowded home reading time was scarce. Her teachers for the most part had been kind and considerate and her brothers and sisters all liked attending the School on the Green and spoke of it with affection. Daisy could remember that when she was three years old she resented having to stay at home while her particular playmate, David, went to school. She was so cross about this that one day she followed him there and sat down at a table and busily tried to draw 'pothooks and hangers' on a slate. 'Pothooks and hangers' was the term then used for the simple shapes the little ones copied to prepare them for writing at a later stage. She was quickly spotted by the teacher and ignominiously returned home where her worried mother had been frantically searching for her.

Of course, there had been days when things had not gone well at school. The day, for example, when her teacher, exasperated beyond bearing by the noisiness and inattention of the children, told the class: 'The next girl who speaks will receive the cane.' She had expected the victim, if there were one, to be one of the usual trouble-makers. Unfortunately it was Daisy. She had become interested in something she was doing and could not keep her enthusiasm to herself. Alas, her voice was clearly heard in the now silent schoolroom. The teacher looked up: 'Who spoke?' Daisy turned bright red and was just about to raise her hand when a school-mate who disliked her called out 'It was Daisy, Miss, it was Daisy!' 'Was it you, Daisy?' 'Yes Miss.' 'Come here.' The child reluctantly rose and went to the front of the class where she was instructed to hold out her hand. She did so and received three stinging cuts. The teacher was as upset as her pupil who had until that time never been in trouble, but having made the promise to cane the next offender she had to carry out her threat or lose some of her authority.

When she came out of school that day Daisy waited for her younger sister, Rhoda. She poured out the story of her disgrace and punishment. 'It was terrible standing there in front of the class, that was as bad as the pain and some of the girls were glad, I know they were. Miss told Mabel off for telling tales, but I still got the cane.'

Rhoda was upset; she loved Daisy and looked up to her. How could anyone cane her beloved sister? 'Will you tell Mother?' she asked. 'Yes' said Daisy: 'But only when I'm alone with her.'

Later when Daisy was able to get her mother to herself for a few minutes she told the story of her disgrace. Hannah listened and then said quietly 'Well you deserved it. You were told not to talk.' 'Oh Mother, I thought you'd understand. I didn't mean to.' 'No but you did and your teacher had no alternative – if ever you become a teacher yourself you must always keep to your word.' Daisy knew her mother was right but she was never to forget the pain and indignity of being caned in front of the class.

The school was – and still is – situated in a rather lovely spot on a green on the edge of Epping Forest. In those days, the older boys were housed on one side of the building and the older girls on the other; in the infants the boys and girls were together. The playground was also divided into two by iron railings, boys on one side, girls on the other. Through the railings the boys watched the girls and, of course, the girls the boys. One boy, watching the girls play, particularly noticed a bright lively youngster named Daisy, who, many years later, became his wife. Daisy, however, could not remember anything about Richard Hardy at that time.

The school catered for a large area. Many of the children had to walk long distances to get there. Richard, for instance, lived over a mile away at the bottom of a long hill. At that period there was no public transport which the children could use, so the only way to school was on foot. They would arrive tired and, on wet days, soaked, after their long walk. There were no school dinners; if the children were to have any lunch at midday they either went home or brought something with them. If they needed a drink there was always the tap in the playground with its metal drinking mug on the end of a long chain. Daisy and her siblings always went home at lunchtime as they only lived five minutes' walk away.

Of all the schools in the Woodford district, at that time, the Green Boys' School had the worst reputation. Whether the boys were under-disciplined, or, maybe, over-disciplined, it is hard to say, but their behaviour left much to be desired. The School Managers often criticised the boys' side of the school where truancy was rife and educational standards generally rather low. Because of this and poor reports by the Schools Inspectors, in some years the education authorities paid a lower grant per boy to the school than that paid to any of the other schools in the district. There were also complaints in the local newspaper about the boys – unpleasant complaints of their robbing nests and throwing the baby birds at one another as well as other unruly behaviour. Richard could remember boys being publicly thrashed in the school for truancy, though seemingly without producing any improvement. Nevertheless, Daisy's brother, David, acquired a relatively good basic education at the Green School which he was able to build on, after he had left school and gone to work. Richard, too, although he left school at the age of 12, had received a reasonable basic education and also the desire to study further. So, despite no doubt valid criticism, the boys' school was certainly not without merit.

But although the boys' side of the school had a poor reputation, this was not so for the girls' department. Perhaps the standards reached were not quite as high as those at, say, Churchfields in South Woodford, where the children gained outside prizes and won scholarships to higher grade schools; but that may have been because the children came from better homes with more ambitious parents. Nevertheless the girls at the Green School were happy there and they were certainly, at least, taught the basic subjects well.

Daisy's younger sister, Rhoda, a bright child who did eventually become a teacher herself, could remember one occasion when she finished the work set for the class long before anyone else and, becoming bored, tried to draw a chicken. She suddenly heard the teacher coming up behind her and put her

12

hand over the picture in the vain hope that 'Miss' would not see. In fact 'Miss' had seen and, sitting down beside the child, gently took her hand from her drawing and then explained where she was going wrong and the best way to set about it. When she grew older, Rhoda became a very good amateur artist and perhaps the encouragement of the teacher those many years earlier had helped.

The children were taught singing by the tonic sol-fa method and, as Rhoda both loved and had a good ear for music, she became very proficient at reading it this way. Daisy too had an extremely good ear for music. At home they had a small harmonium organ, a very poor instrument with the top notes missing, but she managed to pick out hymn tunes on it and if the notes were not there she would just thump the wood and imagine the sound. She had on one occasion played a hymn or two in the church hall and so impressed a local pianist that he offered to give her lessons. Throughout her life, piano playing remained one of her greatest pleasures. She could still play 'by ear' at the age of 96, although by then almost blind.

In the village there were two orphanages for girls, and the children from these homes used to attend the village school with all the other local children. It was believed that one of the orphanages was superior to the other. One of the inmates of the better home was in Daisy's class, a weak little thing who would obviously not be able to go into service, almost the only occupation open to these girls. Those in charge of that orphanage were very concerned that Elizabeth might not be able to support herself, so they made arrangements for her to be taught fine needlework. This was a considerable concession and did enable the girl to keep herself in later life. Another girl, this time from the home with the poorer reputation, was coloured. She was, however completely accepted and well liked by all the village children and added to their enjoyment because wherever she had lived previously she had learnt a lot of the more unusual skipping games and these she taught to her playmates at school.

Girls, of course, had to be instructed in those subjects that would prove suitable to their station in life. Consequently they learnt quite intricate needlework and dressmaking, starting with the most simple stitches and progressing to the really complicated ones. All the girls had to learn how to patch. Most of them would have large families and children's clothes always needed mending. They had to do a top sewn patch, a felled patch and an example of darning. These demonstration pieces of material were beautifully sewn.

As an exercise, the older girls all made camisoles from white cotton. The garments were shapeless but beautifully stitched. There were tiny tucks down the front and the neck and sleeves were finished with a delicate crocheted or knitted edging. The stitches on the seams were tiny. If the girls made them too large the teacher pulled out the cotton and it had to be done again. Rhoda delighted in this work. Daisy did not; she did enough to get

13

by, but never really enjoyed needlework or dressmaking, seeing it as a chore that had to be done. Rhoda made a nightdress while she was still at school. This was much the same as the camisole but longer, and had beautifully made buttonholes down the front and a dainty little collar with feather stitching.

The knitting of socks was also important. Husbands and children wore them out quickly; wives and mothers must know how to knit and supply their families with new ones. During the knitting lessons, a good reader was chosen to read to the class from a story book and this made the lesson more enjoyable. Daisy did not like knitting but she did enjoy reading, and when the teacher was looking round the class it would be her hand that shot up first. 'Please may I read, Miss?' and it would be a very disappointed Daisy if the reply was: 'No, you are too behind with your work.' Quite often, though, she was chosen, as she was a fluent reader with a very pleasant voice.

Marks were given for the completed garments. Ten out of ten was almost unobtainable. Rhoda's niece was shown some of the garments that had been kept by her aunt over the years. They seemed to be perfect in every way but none had achieved the elusive ten out of ten. Rhoda made up her mind that she really would manage to get this magic mark for a pair of socks she had to knit. They were beautifully done but when the headmistress examined them, she said that one sock was a fraction longer than the other, so it was only nine out of ten. Rhoda always said that the headmistress must have pulled the sock, because when the family examined the pair they could not decide which was the longer.

There was always a ready market for the clothing made at school. The materials were of good quality and all the clothes were well made. Most of the girls bought their own. They had to pay only a few pence for them, just enough to cover the cost. Occasionally, however, the few pence were too much for some parents, or they did not want the garments. The camisoles and nightdresses fitted a range of sizes but children's socks were different. Some of the girls took so long to knit them that by the time they were completed their brother or sister had grown too big for them.

Though Rhoda was so good at the intricate stitches she had been taught at school, when she made a blouse or dress she never bothered about such an unimportant thing as the fit of the garment. She would put in exquisite stitching and finish it off perfectly but, when worn, it would look abominable. Lily, her young sister, on the other hand, had a flair for making attractive clothes which fitted well, but she did not bother much about the stitches. The result however was much more acceptable than poor Rhoda's.

A few months before the Second World War, Daisy's daughter told her Aunt Rhoda about one of her friends who was teaching in a local school and had a class of 42 nine-year-olds. Rhoda's answer was very short: 'She's lucky, I taught in that school and I always had 60 children in my class.'

14

Daisy and her brothers and sisters were all taught in these huge classes. In spite of all the difficulties, their spelling, reading, writing and arithmetic were excellent.

Their spelling lessons consisted of repeating the words over and over again. C.A.T. spells cat, C.A.T. spells cat, until they all knew it. As they went through the school the words naturally became harder. With Daisy or her sisters in the house, a dictionary for spelling was unnecessary. There were few words that they could not spell. This was not always good for their children. All they had to do when they wanted to know how to spell a word was to call out 'Mum how do you spell . . . ?' She always knew.

However, Daisy always found the reading lessons difficult. The children used to read a paragraph each in turn. It was all right when there were good readers, but, when it was the turn of a poor one, Daisy found herself reading on to find out what happened next in the story. One day she got engrossed in the book and when the teacher called her name, she had no idea where she was supposed to be reading and started a page ahead of the correct place. Luckily for her this only brought a rather scathing comment from her teacher, who secretly must have had considerable sympathy for the girl. This method of teaching reading must have been difficult and tedious for the teacher, but with 60 children there was no other way of ensuring that everyone had read. The slow ones found it difficult to follow and the bright pupils got tired of waiting.

History and geography lessons consisted of learning lists by heart. There were lists of rivers, counties, countries and dates. Dates of battles, of Kings of England, etc. One day, many years later, Daisy watched her little grandson trying to draw a map of the district in which he lived. She was fascinated. 'What a lovely way to learn geography. I wish they had taught us like that! I knew all the rivers of England but I couldn't draw a map of the district round my home.'

Daisy's ambition to be a teacher may have been stimulated by her being one of the older children in the family. She must often have acted as teacher and nursemaid to her younger sisters. She would do her best to smooth their paths in life if she could and it was she who told them the 'facts of life'. One day she had found blood on her clothes; no one had told her what happened at the onset of puberty. She was petrified; she must be bleeding to death, what terrible illness had got her in its grip? She was almost too terrified to ask her mother what was wrong, but in the end she plucked up her courage and did so, and then, belatedly, her mother explained. Daisy was determined that her younger sisters should not suffer similar distress and made sure that they knew what was in store for them before it happened.

The inconvenience of the 'period' to women and girls of that time was considerable. They had none of the modern products. Instead lengths of terry towelling or other absorbent cloths were cut up into suitable sizes and, after use, soaked in cold water and then boiled. During the time her 'period' was on, no girl was allowed to take a bath, and if an unhappy girl happened to pick that time for a holiday at the seaside she must on no account paddle. Dreadful diseases were forecast should a girl disobey this rule.

At the start of that new school year Daisy felt extremely hopeful; she was 13 and her life lay before her. She was sure that at the end of the year she would become a pupil teacher and then, finally, a teacher. She was excited at the prospect. It would be so much more interesting than the few other openings for girls of her class. The only cloud on the horizon was that another girl was also hoping to become a pupil teacher the following year and she, too, like Daisy, was on a form of probation. Mary came from a more favoured home. It was unlikely that both girls would be accepted. Daisy put this thought behind her. She was sure she would prove herself more able than Mary; she was determined to.

Pupil teacher places were not granted for merit alone. Influence and family background had a great pull. Daisy's friend, Christine, who was to become her brother David's sister-in-law, was not clever, yet, mainly because she was well dressed and came from a more acceptable family, was encouraged to become a pupil teacher although she had no real wish to do so. Although she attended the pupil teacher centre for several years she did not complete the course and never taught.

3
Esther and Aubrey

That autumn Daisy was considered almost 'grown up' by her younger sisters. She was not really at school in the way they were; she was 'helping teacher' with the little ones and so her sisters looked up to her. At home she was considered her mother's chief assistant and was a competent help in the Coffee House and with the other children. Hannah could not imagine how she would have managed without Daisy. Ada was in service and Hannah needed far more help than she ever was able to obtain. The trouble now was Esther's health, which had started to deteriorate rapidly. Most of the time the little girl had to remain in bed and she suffered almost continuous pain. The child had contracted rheumatic fever when very young and had been left with a severely damaged heart.

Daisy's coming home from school was a bright spot in the little girl's day.

Either Daisy would look after the shop for a while making it possible for Muzzy, as Esther called Hannah, to sit with her suffering daughter, or else Daisy would sit with the child, amusing her with stories or hymn tunes on the old harmonium.

With the onset of the cold, dark and damp days of winter, poor Esther's health deteriorated further and Daisy, running up to greet her after returning from school, would be distressed to see how weak and frail the little girl looked. She would endeavour to think up all the most amusing stories about school to tell her, until the child, forgetting her pain for a little while, would brighten and look better.

Although Alfred, their father, was generally a harsh and domineering person, of whom the children were afraid, he endeavoured to make Christmas an enjoyable family holiday and his character seemed to change at this time. Because of this and the fact that the Coffee House was closed for Christmas Day, the children always looked forward to Christmas.

On Christmas Eve, Aunt Susannah came to stay for the holiday and looked after Esther and Lily, while Daisy, with her mother's guidance, made cakes and tarts. After the shop shut, Daisy and her mother scrubbed out the big room while Rhoda washed down the tables. Then the tables were pushed against the walls leaving a large space in the middle for games. Esther and Lily had been busily making paper chains and their father had collected greenery and berries from the forest. When David came home from work in the evening he and Alfred decorated the room until it was completely transformed from its usual appearance.

All the children, including David, who, though now working, was only 15, hung up their stockings, or socks, on the rungs at the bottom of the ladder leading to the loft. Alfred and Hannah had collected small inexpensive items, usually sweets, for all their children and on Christmas Eve these were stuffed into the stockings. In every case an apple and orange were pushed into the toe and, just to make the opening operation more hazardous, a few holly leaves would be packed in between the gifts, to prick the urgent fingers of the children as they hunted for the treasures.

But before the children had their stockings they must sleep, and Christmas Eve was the time the Waits came round. All the children loved Christmas carols and those sung by the Waits seemed somehow special. Lying in their cold loft, knowing that their stockings were safely fixed to the bottom of the ladder, the girls waited drowsily hoping to hear the Waits. These were just a group of villagers who went round carol singing every Christmas Eve. But the fact that it was Christmas Eve and tomorrow was Christmas Day, the one day of the year when the shop would be shut and they would be able to have a party and entertain their friends, added to the glamour of the singers, who would have been surprised to learn how anxiously their visit was awaited by the children.

If any of the children fell asleep without hearing the carols, there would be recriminations in the morning. 'Didn't the Waits come last night? I stayed awake ages and didn't hear them.' 'Of course they came, you fell asleep. They sang beautifully, someone even tried a descant.' 'You pig! Why didn't you wake me.' 'I tried to but you were fast asleep.' 'You didn't try hard enough, I shall not enjoy Christmas so much now.' But whether or not they heard the Waits, they still enjoyed Christmas.

Weeks before, the children had helped Hannah in the preparation of the the Christmas pudding, cake and mince pies. Raisins had been stoned, no seedless raisins in those days, nuts blanched and chopped and candied peel cut up finely. This latter job was one which the children enjoyed, as the candied peel was thickly encrusted with sugar. This orange or lemon flavoured sugar could be peeled off and eaten as a delicious sweet.

Breakfast on Christmas Day was a more leisurely meal than usual, although having eaten many of the goodies from the stockings the children were not hungry. Afterwards Hannah put two large chickens to roast in the oven and left the pudding on the top of the stove to bubble the hours happily away. David took his younger sisters for a walk while Daisy stayed with Esther, and Susannah helped Hannah prepare the vegetables and Alfred dozed in front of the stove.

When the Christmas dinner had been eaten and cleared away, and all the family had rested quietly for a while, the tables against the walls in the shop were spread with tarts, cakes, dates, nuts and sandwiches, which Daisy, her mother, and Aunt Susannah had prepared, and the family were now ready to welcome their friends into their home. This in itself was a great event. The Coffee House, in order to fulfil its purpose, had to remain open weekdays, Saturdays and bank holidays, all the year round, until well into the evening. Indeed often the busiest days of the year were those when other people were on holiday. Sometimes on bank holidays, people, coming out from London in brakes for days in the country, would call at the Coffee House for refreshments. This, though welcomed for the extra money it brought, also brought much back-breaking work. Of course, normally in such an environment it would have been impossible for the family to have a party. On Sundays the Coffee House was closed, but Hannah's and Alfred's religious convictions would not have permitted them to have a party in their home on that day.

Christmas, however, was different. The shop was shut and the family were able to entertain their friends to a party. The shop was an ideal place for this purpose with plenty of space for games. Daisy was able to play tunes on the harmonium and they would have a sing-song. Most of the friends would be from church and school and they enjoyed singing carols.

One Christmas, however, Esther was very ill and could not take part in any of the games. Although enjoying herself immensely, Daisy was very conscious of her young sister who had been brought downstairs and placed in a comfortable chair, in a warm spot, where she could see all the others.

Daisy watched her anxiously and, after a while, noticed that she was obviously in pain but did not want to spoil the pleasure of the others. The older girl touched her brother David on the arm, 'Will you help me get Esther upstairs, please? Mother and Aunt Susannah have gone to wish their friends a happy Christmas. They won't be long, but Etty seems in such pain and looks so tired.' David was only too willing to help. 'She is only such a little thing, I think I can carry her up myself.' David had left school two years earlier and was now working as an office boy in London. In his spare time he was studying hard and hoped to take the examination to enable him to enter the Post Office. He quietly helped Esther over to the stairs, then, with Daisy following behind, carried her up to their parents' bedroom where, for the present she was sleeping.

Daisy helped her young sister to undress and settled her into bed. However, before she lay down Etty put her arms round her older sister. 'Thanks for looking after me, the pain is so bad but I didn't want to worry anyone.' Daisy asked if it was too bad for Esther to enjoy Christmas. The child replied, 'Not all the time, I loved being with everyone. It gets lonely sometimes up here on my own.' The child went on to say that the pain was often so bad that she did not know how to bear it. 'Oh Daisy, I don't want to stay here in pain, I want to go home to Jesus.' Daisy could not bear her beloved sister talking like that and said that she was sure the doctor would be able to make her well. 'Are you?', answered Esther, 'I'm not, I don't seem to be getting better at all.'

Daisy stayed with her little sister and sang some carols softly. Then, as the child became more relaxed, Hannah entered the room. She thanked Daisy for taking care of Esther and added that she had been afraid it would be rather too much excitement for the child. She added that Esther had so very much wanted to be part of this year's Christmas celebrations. There was sadness in Hannah's words as if she knew it would be the child's last Christmas with them all. She sent Daisy downstairs to join in the party fun. Daisy went downstairs slowly and sadly, she was very upset and did not feel she wanted to join in the fun any more. Etty was such a pretty little thing. She was also quite clever and did well at school when she was able to go. It seemed unfair that she was unable to enjoy life. She couldn't be going to die, not her little Etty. She was quiet for a while when she joined the others, but later began to enjoy herself once more.

After Christmas that year, the weather became very cold indeed. There was frost day and night and the local ponds soon became deeply frozen. The coldness of the weather, however, did not seem to affect the ability of Alfred's hens to lay and one Saturday morning Daisy and her younger sister Rhoda, were sent out on the usual, and to them, distasteful, job of selling the eggs. As they passed the local pond the two sisters saw that their friends had made a long slide and were going down it one after the other. They called to Daisy and Rhoda to join them. Daisy could not resist the temptation of joining in with her friends. 'Don't be silly', said Rhoda, 'You'll probably fall over and break the eggs.' 'Don't worry, I'll be careful', Daisy called back to her sister. She joined the queue of children and took her turn on the slide. She managed beautifully and returned to Rhoda. 'It's good fun come and join us, I'm going to have another go.' The more cautious Rhoda declined to join her sister who, this time, when she came to the end of the slide, lost her footing and she, and the eggs, went sprawling.

Daisy picked herself up and looked at the eggs lying in a yellow mess on the ice. Every one had come out of the basket and all were smashed. The girl picked up the basket. She was nearly in tears, but was not going to cry in front of her friends. 'Father will be furious', she said, 'I don't want to go home'. Rhoda, who also had a basket of eggs said 'Let's sell the ones I have, then I'll go home and say you are coming later. I'll try to get mother on her own and explain what has happened. I am sure she'll understand and help.' So the two sisters walked conscientiously around the village and managed to dispose of all the remaining eggs. Rhoda then hurried home, handed the money to her father and explained that Daisy would be coming later. She then managed to get her mother aside and explained what had happened. Hannah always tried to keep a small store of money hidden away on which she could call in an emergency. On this occasion she decided that an upset between Daisy and her father would worry Esther and, anyway, Hannah had sympathy for her older daughter, she could understand her wanting to join in the fun with her friends and knew how little chance she had to do so. She went to her secret store and gave Rhoda the money Daisy would have earned if she had sold the eggs instead of breaking them, and Daisy was able to hand it to her father, who never learned of the accident to his precious merchandise.

Later Hannah took Daisy aside and told her how foolish she had been and what good sense Rhoda had shown in resisting the temptation to slide. Daisy was very sorry as she knew how scarce money was. As she had got older she had come to realise that despite all the hard work, the Coffee House was making very little money. There had been some days when the total amount taken had not been more than half a crown. No wonder their father had tried to augment the income in other ways. Daisy told her mother she would do extra jobs in the shop and home to pay back the money. Her mother laughingly replied that she was already a great help and that she wished that all her children were able to enjoy themselves more often. She then told Daisy that they would now forget all about the accident.

How the children loathed those eggs! Whenever they saw a basketful they shuddered. It was all right when they could eat them themselves, and it was a good thing they had them for Esther, but when it came to hawking them around the village, they hated it.

There had been an occasion a year or so previously when the sisters had not been able to sell a single egg. Again they were terribly afraid of their father's anger and, again, their mother came to their rescue. On this occasion their oldest sister was at home helping her mother who, therefore, was able to leave the Coffee House. Hannah immediately put on her bonnet and coat, and she and the girls together went round the houses again until they had managed to dispose of all the eggs. Their mother, whenever possible, stood between the children and their father's anger.

As winter slowly turned into spring, little Esther became weaker. Daisy spent more and more time with her as the child was in great pain and needed constant help and comfort. The doctor said Esther must have buttermilk and this was given to them free by the wife of a local farmer. But neither the buttermilk, nor the eggs, nor the loving care she was given, helped the little girl regain her health.

Hannah had always been a religious woman and the children had gone regularly to Church and Sunday School. Esther, remarkably for a child so young, had no fear of death, in fact she appeared to want it. The pain rarely left her now and the doctor seemed unable to help. There were times when Etty desperately wanted her mother, when she felt that only Hannah's presence would cause the pain to release its grip and then the little girl would cry out calling 'Muzzie, Muzzie, where are you? Please come', and Hannah would, if possible, leave the Coffee House in someone else's care. Wearied with her work and deeply distressed by her daughter's pain, she would sit beside her suffering child, trying to give her a little comfort and relief.

One day when Daisy was in the room with Etty and thought the child was asleep, she walked over to the window and looked out across the square to the countryside beyond. It looked pleasant in the spring sunshine. Suddenly she heard a queer croaking noise coming from the bed. She walked quickly across and leant over her little sister. She realised that Etty was trying to sing her favourite hymn, 'There's a home for little children above the bright blue sky' Daisy, nearly in tears, asked Etty if she would like her to sing it. The child nodded and Daisy sang it through and the little girl seemed to gain some comfort from the hymn. She obviously had a picture of a heaven where she would be happy and free from pain and able to play like other children.

Very shortly after this Esther died. Her death made a deep impression on all the family. Hannah was heartbroken. The poor woman was pregnant at the time with what would be her last child, and did not feel well herself. She now had to arrange the funeral, which was going to be a costly affair for them, even though they would keep it as simple as possible. Certain wealthier members of the community who respected Hannah came to her help with monetary aid and gifts.

Esther was placed in her coffin, with the lid removed, in the darkened parlour upstairs, and there all the children were brought in to say goodbye to their little sister. The sight of her in that coffin in the dim room, remained with them all for the rest of their lives.

In fact, the drama of Esther's death carried on into the next generation. All Daisy's children were told the story of little Esther and had looked at the only picture there was of their young aunt. However Daisy's elder daughter, Winifred, had another experience which showed the depth of her grandmother's sorrow for her daughter. Winifred was eight years old, her grandmother 76. Daisy now lived next door to Lily and there was a lot of coming and going between the two families. For ease of access, a little gate had been made in the fence between the two houses.

Hannah was living with Lily at the time, and was nearing her own death. No one wished her to be left alone but Lily had to go out. Daisy had another daughter a year old as well as a boy of four and a half to look after, and could not sit with her mother. Winifred was therefore told to go and stay with Hannah while Auntie Lily was out shopping. This she did and found her grandmother talking to herself. The child did not realise how very ill the old lady was. In fact Hannah was dying and did not really know what she was doing. She picked up a cushion and cradled it in her arms. Her grandchild joined in the 'game' and learned that the cushion was Esther and she was in pain and had to be comforted. The old lady and the young child gently placed 'Esther' on a chair, wrapped her up warmly because she was so ill, and together they nursed her until Lily came back and the child was sent home.

When Daisy's daughter, an elderly lady herself, recalled the incident, it was not with distress. She vividly remembered how she herself thought it was a game and felt that she might have been able to help her grandmother by the acceptance of 'Esther' whereas an adult would have been too distressed and embarrassed.

One thing that distressed Hannah greatly was that she did not have a good photograph of Esther. The only one in existence was taken when Esther was well enough to go to school. All the children were going to have their photographs taken and had been told to go to school dressed in their best clothes. Most of the children at that time wore elaborate pinafores covering their dresses. Esther had asked her mother to let her wear a clean, nearly new pinafore which had been beautifully made for her by Aunt Susannah. The child went to school thinking that she really looked rather nice. However, before the photograph was taken, the teacher issued the decree that all children must take off their pinafores. Esther pleaded with the teacher to be allowed to keep hers on, but to no avail. She had to remove hers like all the other children. Consequently when the photograph was taken she was in a bad temper, and it showed. So the only photograph in existence of Esther showed the little girl pouting, a thing she rarely did.

As was a custom of the times, despite the fact that money was so scarce, all the children were given little silver lockets with a piece of Esther's hair inside. These were treasured and kept until, some years later, thieves broke into the Coffee House and ransacked the place and, of course, among the treasures taken were the mourning lockets.

Because there was no good picture of Esther, Hannah decided she must have photographs taken of all her other children. After all, Rhoda was not very strong. So after the funeral, all the children, dressed in deep mourning, were taken to the photographer's studio to have their picture taken, and a very stilted picture it was too.

The expense of Esther's funeral was so great that Hannah wondered what would happen if any of the other children died. In view of this she took out funeral insurance of one penny a week for each of them, which sometimes she had considerable difficulty finding, but nevertheless, it lifted one worry from her shoulders.

One life had been lost, another was about to commence. Daisy's youngest brother, Aubrey, was born a few months later. His birth, though giving Hannah a great deal of work, probably helped ease the pain of Esther's death a little. Alfred was delighted that the latest baby should be a boy and indeed Hannah also no doubt preferred to have another son. A girl would never have replaced her beloved Esther. Although there was already another son in the family, Alfred, for some reason, never showed him much affection, but used him as a labourer. As soon as David could push the iron shod wheelbarrow, it had been his job to trundle it laden to and from the allotment, which was at the bottom of a long hill. This was a terrible strain on the young growing boy and probably damaged his heart. For Aubrey, however, nothing was too good. The girls were expected to be his nursemaids and he was decidedly spoilt.

When young, Aubrey was far from strong. He too had rheumatic fever and the doctor said that if he were to survive he would have to spend a whole year quietly at home resting. He was just about four years old at the time and though not medically strong he had a lively and enquiring mind and enjoyed being the centre of attention. None of the other members of the family forgot that year. The sisters read to him and even their father helped sometimes playing games of snakes and ladders or draughts with the little boy. Rhoda was a pupil teacher by then, with very little free time. Ada was away in service and Lily at school all day, so most of the nursing had to be done by Daisy. In later years Aubrey always spoke of her as his good nurse.

At this time, there was a legal requirement to have children vaccinated, and there had been sporadic cases of smallpox in the area. Alfred did not want this as he did not think Aubrey was strong enough. The doctor, however, said that the danger of the disease was much greater than Aubrey's weakness and the fact that the child was resting most of the time would help him get over the vaccination easily. The doctor, against Alfred's wishes, vaccinated Aubrey. Alfred was furious and directly the doctor had left the house, sucked the vaccine from the child's arm. A week or so later when the doctor found that the vaccination had not taken he revaccinated the child; again his father sucked out the vaccine. Next time the doctor visited Aubrey he was dismayed to find that there was again no vaccination pustule on his arm; he thought that the child must have a natural immunity but decided to try once more. A third time Alfred sucked out the vaccine – or tried to – but this time he failed and Aubrey was at last successfully vaccinated – to his father's indignation and the doctor's satisfaction.

Aubrey knew he was his father's favourite and enjoyed being the centre of attention, and whenever Daisy appeared, whatever she was doing, he would start wheedling. 'Daisy dear, will you read me a story? – I like listening to you read.' He would keep on until in the end he got his way and Daisy would have to stop what she was doing and read to him. By this time there were a good many children's books in the home, most of course highly moral. Every year throughout their days at day and Sunday schools all the children regularly won prizes and these prizes were always books. Aubrey's favourite, however, was *Little Folks*. This was not a prize, but a children's paper, published weekly, and someone had presented the children with some bound volumes of the magazine. There were stories of magic and adventure; stories written by children for children, rhymes and puzzles, and all kinds of interesting articles. Indeed not only did *Little Folks* give pleasure to Aubrey but to two further generations of children.

The books the children had received from Sunday School for attendance were very varied. Some were good but others most unsuitable for a young boy. *Buy Your Own Cherries* for example, was the story of the reform of a drunkard, an odd subject but surprisingly interesting. *Ministering Children* on the other hand was exceedingly boring, a long book about children, too good to be true, and their dull 'ministerings' – no one liked that very much. One book Aubrey enjoyed immensely was *The Oliver Children*. This was a story about some small children living in Ireland. After one of them had a bad attack of measles, two of the little girls were sent on their own to stay with an uncle in London. Their grandfather put them on the boat in charge of the stewardess who found a charming young lady to look after them. At Fleetwood this young lady, who was travelling in another direction, put the children in charge of an elderly lady going to London. However, at Crewe the children got out of the train to buy sweets and, of course, the train went without them and the children stood on the platform shouting 'Oh, stop, stop!'. Aubrey always found this immensely funny and would ask for it time and time again.

Esther had won one book and one book only, when she had been at school. That was Totty's *Natural History*. She had loved it, and so did Aubrey. Before he was well it was nearly worn out. There were pictures and stories of frogs, worms, newts and other creatures. None of the words in the book had more than five letters, so it was easy for a bright child to read.

24

Plate 1 – (a) Hannah's grandmother, c 1860; *(b)* Hannah, c 1870; *(c)* Alfred and Hannah, c 1874; *(d)* Aunt Susannah, c 1890; *(e)* Alfred, c 1890; *(f)* Esther, c 1893

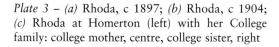

Plate 2 – Rhoda, Daisy and Lily after Esther's death

Plate 3 – *(a)* Rhoda, c 1897; *(b)* Rhoda, c 1904; *(c)* Rhoda at Homerton (left) with her College family: college mother, centre, college sister, right

Plate 4 – Aubrey and Lily, c 1900

Plate 5 – Daisy, c 1904

Plate 6 – A class at the School on the Green (now Woodford Green Primary School), c 1897: Olive, Daisy's sister in law, first girl in the back row; Rhoda, second row from the front, fifth from the left

Plate 7 – Miss Clutton, headmistress of the School on the Green

Aubrey would lie on his bed imagining catching these creatures in the local ponds and planning how he would keep them. When Daisy did not have time to read to him he would look at the pictures in an illustrated Bible and also in a copy of Bunyan's *Pilgrim's Progress*. This latter book had some quite frightening pictures, but he enjoyed looking at them. But the child disliked being on his own and hated not receiving attention. On one occasion poor Daisy had been reading to him for a considerable while and felt entitled to read a little to herself. She had her favourite, *Jane Eyre*, with her and sat down with it in Aubrey's room and was soon engrossed. This was not good enough for Aubrey. 'What are you reading?' Daisy took no notice. He called out louder, 'Daisy dear, read to me'. Daisy replied that she was reading to herself and he wouldn't like the book. 'I would, I would' he shouted in a temper: 'If you don't read to me I'll cry.' Daisy gave up. She read him a passage from *Jane Eyre*. Aubrey found it boring and dropped off to sleep and the girl was allowed a little peace.

However trying the family found Aubrey's enforced year of rest and quietness, it was no doubt the right medicine for him. From that time on he gained in health and strength and had a long and active life.

4
Service

It was a beautiful afternoon, that last day of the summer term, in the year 1895. But Daisy, walking along the sunlit road with the mellow light dancing off the trees, could not see any beauty anywhere. She could only see darkness around her. In her eyes her future was a dark black tunnel with no light at the end. She heard the other children running delightedly home, revelling in their freedom from school for the next few weeks but she did not want to go home. Her hopes for the future had been dashed. For many years she had dreamed of becoming a teacher. There were few opportunities for girls in her walk of life. The careers that began to open up for women were not yet available. Women had not yet been accepted into office work as typists. She did not like needlework and she certainly did not want to go into domestic service like her sister Ada. Another opening would be to work in a shop but that did not appeal to her. She was sure she would have proved a good teacher. She had been able to manage the children easily and was liked by the younger ones. She had always been towards the top of her class.

Why then had she not been given the coveted post of pupil teacher? It was, she was sure, simply because Mary came from a wealthier home, she did not have to sell eggs round the neighbourhood. She was not one of the children from the area 'Behind the Castle' which at that time had a rather bad reputation. Of course Mary could play the piano well, always an asset for a schoolteacher, but then she had a proper piano at home while Daisy had only a very dilapidated instrument on which to practise. Oh why was life so unfair?

Rhoda came running along the road obviously looking for her sister. Suddenly she noticed Daisy sitting disconsolately on the grass and ran over to her. 'Mother wants you, aren't you coming home?' Then seeing the expression on her sister's face asked what was wrong. 'I can't be a teacher, they don't want me', muttered the older girl. 'Oh go home, leave me alone.' Rhoda waited for a moment and then ran off home to break the news to Hannah. Hannah had, however, already learnt the news from the school authorities but had said nothing to Daisy. Alfred had said that it didn't matter because he would never had signed the documents to allow her to be a pupil teacher. Hannah, however, was very well aware of the heartbreak the decision would cause Daisy.

As she wandered slowly home, Daisy wondered what would happen now. Her hopes had been shattered. What were the chances for her younger sisters? She knew in her heart that Rhoda was much quicker at learning than she was. She grasped ideas easily and seemed to know as much as Daisy and yet was two years younger. Would Rhoda have the opportunity that had passed her by? Daisy decided that if it lay within her power she would do all she could to see that her younger sisters would be able to take up some kind of worthwhile career. She knew her mother would give what help she could, but she also knew that her father, autocratic, selfish and sick, would put as many obstacles as he could in the way of his daughters' progress. Though still feeling hurt and bitter at fate, when she reached home she squared her shoulders and decided she would at least do what she could to help the others achieve a better life than lay ahead for herself.

She reached the Coffee House and went in to find her mother. She poured out all her troubles. Hannah, knowing how much the ambition had meant to Daisy was very sympathetic but finally added: 'Never mind dear, I have always enjoyed having you near me, and I really do need help. Let's run the shop together shall we?' Daisy's face brightened, 'Oh Mum, what would I do without you?'

The future for Daisy now appeared to be helping her mother in the Coffee House. However, before this happened, another event occurred which was in some ways even more traumatic for Daisy. Mrs Robertson, the local bank manager's wife, had heard that Daisy had not been chosen for the place of pupil teacher. It was difficult for some employers to find good domestic staff, and Mrs Robertson was known as a poor employer.

However she carried some influence in the area and she needed someone to come to live in her house and work as a housemaid. She asked Hannah if Daisy could come for the time being. Hannah was put in a difficult position. She knew that Mrs Robertson despised her domestic staff and was horrified at the thought of Daisy working for her. On the other hand it was important not to offend such a person, so, without consulting Daisy, she agreed. She found her daughter and told her that on the following Monday she would be starting at the Robertsons. 'Oh no, mother, not that! I couldn't. Oh please, not that!' and she burst out sobbing. Her mother, though sympathetic, was adamant. She could not afford to offend anyone of any importance in the village, and she had just learnt that Daisy's older sister, Ada, was leaving her job and would be coming home for a while. Therefore, Daisy would not, after all, really be needed in the shop.

Daisy rushed away from her home, found a quiet spot on the green, threw herself down on the grass and wept bitterly. She knew she'd really been quite brave when she had learnt of the failure of her teaching hopes, but how could she face the future now? Her mother had let her down. Life had let her down. There was nothing to live for. She had always hated the thought of domestic service and she had never liked Mrs Robertson who, she was sure, despised the Ensom family. After a while she quietened and lay still and the peace of her surroundings crept into her. She rose and walked quietly back home.

As she entered the kitchen her mother, who felt with good reason that she had lost her daughter's trust, looked up and said: 'Cheer up, Daisy, you need not stay there long if you don't like it. When Ada finds another job I promise that if you are still unhappy you shall come home.' She went on to say that although Mrs Robertson was perhaps a rather difficult woman to work for, she also had her share of troubles. Her only son was consumptive and very ill. However, Daisy replied that her mother had far more to worry about, she had the shop to run, a young baby to look after, a husband who was unwell and they had lost darling Esther but she was still pleasant to others, unlike Mrs Robertson. 'Oh well', responded Hannah, 'We don't have to worry about keeping up appearances, and Mrs Robertson feels that she must always make a show to keep her place in the community.'

Ada returned home. Unlike Daisy she was content to go into service and had had several good employers. However in her last position she had been unhappy for various reasons and her mother had agreed that she should come home for a while. Ada hoped that soon she would be able to get a better job in a much nicer house. This made Daisy feel better. If Ada were not at home then surely she would be able to return and help her mother. She was sure that she would be better able to look after the younger ones than her sister. She could now see a little ray of light ahead and therefore decided to make the best of her time at the Robertsons. She might be able to learn something useful there.

Daisy was allowed more freedom than usual and by the time Monday came felt decidedly better. After all, here was a challenge and it was up to her to face it. She was also aware that her grandmother had done very well in domestic service, rising to the important post of housekeeper. She also had heard that her grandmother was helping Ada to find a better post. Although she had no desire to copy her grandmother, Daisy decided that she would show everyone that if she really wanted to she could get to the top whatever she had to do.

Hannah had been told that Daisy would have to wear a black frock and white apron when serving at table in the evening. The black frock the girl had worn for Esther's funeral was considered suitable – Daisy secretly considered it very suitable as the job represented the death of her ambitions.

On Monday morning at 8 o'clock Daisy presented herself at the side entrance of the Robertsons' house. She knocked somewhat timidly and the door was opened by a cheerful, fresh-faced young lady, who greeted Daisy warmly. Ethel was the other maid living in the house and she did most of the cooking under the supervision of Mrs Robertson. The only outside help they had was with the laundry, otherwise the two girls had to do all the housework between them. As Ethel's work was mainly concerned with the kitchen and cooking, Daisy was expected to look after the rest of the house.

Mrs Robertson was not a good employer. She did not think the 'lower orders' merited any consideration at all. They had been put on the earth to pander to people like herself. Her aim in life was to get as much work as she could out of her maids while paying them as little as possible. The girls shared a double bed in an attic room at the top of the house and all the water they needed for their ablutions had to be carried up three flights of stairs. It would be extremely cold in winter and the bedclothes were rather thin. Both girls were kept working hard all day and late into the evening. On one occasion, Daisy, who thought all her jobs for the day were finished, was sitting down in the kitchen reading a favourite book she had brought with her. She had been reading for only about five minutes when her employer walked in. On finding the girl so occupied Mrs Robertson scolded her soundly. No one in such a menial position should enjoy reading. She was told curtly to shut her book and cut up paper for use in the lavatory and Mrs Robertson added she did not expect to find Daisy reading in her house again.

Unfortunately, though Mrs Robertson wished others to believe she belonged to the upper classes, her resources were inadequate for her requirements. If she gave a dinner party, the food and drink would be lavish for that meal only and then, for the rest of the week, the household would have to live on the barest minimum. This imposed a severe strain on Ethel's catering and on the living standards of the two maids. Ethel told Daisy cheerfully that she did not intend staying long, and, as soon as something 'turned up' she would leave. Daisy hoped nothing would turn up for some time, as she enjoyed Ethel's company on the few occasions they were free together.

Ethel was a cheerful young lady, determined to look on the bright side of life, and she was also an excellent mimic. She could see humour in any situation, so that often when Daisy would normally have been depressed by the way things were turning out, Ethel would have her laughing instead. A friendship grew up between the two girls – Daisy felt she would not be able to bear it at the Robertsons if Ethel left. Ethel was far more phlegmatic in her approach to life. If Daisy left, then another maid would come, and Ethel, from past experience, knew that she could make friends with almost anyone, in this respect she was very lucky. As it was, the two girls cooperated well making a good team, and, despite herself, Mrs Robertson was impressed.

The task Daisy hated most was whitening the steps. Kneeling on the steps in front of the house, with a whitening block in her hands, a sacking apron over her skirt, and a pail of cold water at her side, she could see her erstwhile schoolmates going by. Instead of being a teacher she was cleaning the steps of the Robertsons' house. What could be more humiliating? Probably none of the girls realised what Daisy was thinking. After all most of them would probably end up doing that kind of work. But to Daisy, that chore of step-whitening was the worst indignity life could offer her.

However, once the step-whitening was completed, Daisy felt happier. Inside the house she could no longer be seen and looked down upon by her former friends. Blackleading the grates was another chore she hated, but on the other hand she certainly liked to see the bright gleaming grates afterwards. Daisy had always appreciated neatness and cleanliness, and, from that point of view, she did not really mind the work.

Above all, she enjoyed cleaning and polishing the beautiful silver and, afterwards, if there were a dinner party, setting the table with the crisply laundered tablecloths and napery and sparkling glasses and silverware. She learnt that every item of cutlery and glassware had to be correctly placed and when, finally, the table had been arranged correctly, she would stand in front of it entranced. To her it was a glimpse of fairyland, a land she never expected to enter but which she now was privileged to view from the outside. The pictures on the walls also fascinated her and while cleaning a room, she would make up stories about them, which, if not too tired, she would sometimes tell Ethel in bed.

Daisy was able to go home sometimes for a couple of hours and, as yet, Ada was still there. Ada did not want to live at home permanently. She had lived away for several years and on her return to the Coffee House had found her father very difficult. She was now 19, an age when many of her contemporaries had married, but, on the one occasion she had been asked to walk out with a young man and had started to cross The Square with him, her father had erupted from the Coffee House and shouted to the girl to come home. Ada was frightened of her father and meekly left her friend and returned home. Her father said she must never walk out with a young man without his permission again. Ada was hoping that an offer of employment would come quickly; she loved her mother but felt she could not stay in the same place as her father.

Daisy begged her mother to let her come home as soon as Ada left. Hannah looked down at her young daughter, at the weariness round her eyes, and at her chapped hands. 'I'll come and see Mrs Robertson shortly. As soon as I know when Ada is leaving I'll ask Mrs Robertson to let you come home. I know she has been very pleased with you and will not want to lose you.' Daisy however muttered that Mrs Robertson had not given her that impression and that she never seemed pleased about anything.

Mrs Robertson's only son, Charles, was consumptive, and seriously ill. In fact the doctors gave no hope of his recovery. Daisy used to hear him coughing and felt very sorry for him. If she ever met him round the house, he looked flushed and seemed almost too tired to walk. He was quite pleasant to the two maids and, though sometimes irritable, usually spoke kindly to them. Daisy was always happy to carry out any errands he needed.

One day when Charles was confined to bed and appeared unable to eat any food, his mother came down to the kitchen and asked Ethel to prepare a poached egg and take it to his room. Ethel cooked the egg but in doing so broke the yolk. 'Never mind', she thought, ' It will still taste the same.' She laid a tray prettily and took the egg up to Charles' room. Charles took one look at it and said: 'Take that away, the look of it makes me feel sick.' At that moment Mrs Robertson came into the room. She looked disgustedly at the tray. 'That is no meal for an invalid, take it away, Ethel, and if you are unable to poach an egg properly, ask Daisy to do it.' Ethel returned to the kitchen and found Daisy sitting by the fire and explained what had happened. 'You know it's funny, Daisy, but for some reason I can never poach an egg properly.'

Daisy asked if she should poach the egg. Ethel accepted Daisy's offer, but said that they should share the broken one between them first. After all one of Mrs Robertson's sayings was 'Waste not, want not'.

Daisy poached an egg perfectly and was laying the tray just as her employer came into the room. She looked at the egg, and for once thanked Daisy and said that if Charles asked for a poached egg again she was to cook it. Ethel did not mind; as she said: 'One less job for me and one more for you.' Daisy explained to her friend about her young sister, Esther, and how often all she could eat had been a poached egg. As the child had no appetite for food they had needed to tempt her to eat and Daisy had done quite a lot of the special invalid cooking.

Shortly after that incident Ethel heard of another job, for which she applied. She told Daisy that she intended to take it if it were offered to her. Immediately she had some free time Daisy ran home and told her mother.

Hannah said that as Ada would be leaving very soon she would go over and see Mrs Robertson that day and explain that she needed to have Daisy with her. Alfred's health had deteriorated again and Aubrey was quite a difficult child to handle. She would definitely require Daisy's help.

Daisy went back to the Robertsons and told Ethel what her Mother had said. While Daisy had been out Ethel had learnt that she had got the job subject to a good report from Mrs Robertson. With her heart in her mouth the girl approached her employer and told her that she had found another position but would need a reference. To her surprise, Mrs Robertson was quite pleasant and said of course she would give Ethel a good reference and then wished her well in her new post. Ethel reported this conversation to Daisy and added: 'You could have knocked me down with a feather, she was really quite nice.'

Hannah, as she had promised, went to see Daisy's employer who, through the local grapevine, had already learnt of Ada's impending departure and thus had expected Daisy to return home. Consequently, Mrs Robertson had made arrangements for a young girl from one of the orphanages to come and work for her as soon as Daisy left.

Mrs Robertson called Daisy into her sitting room and told her that she would be free to return home as soon as the girl from the orphanage arrived. Then, for the first time since the girl had been in the house, expressed appreciation for her help. Daisy was surprised. It was so unlike Mrs Robertson. Her employer told the girl how pleased Charles had been with her invalid cooking. Daisy explained that she had often cooked for Esther when her mother was busy and said that she hoped the young master would soon get better. 'I am afraid that will never be', replied his mother, and Daisy felt very sad for her. She herself knew what it was like to lose someone you loved dearly and Charles was Mrs Robertson's only son.

It seemed to Ethel and Daisy that their mistress had been softened by the deterioration in her son's health. There seemed to be a different atmosphere around the house and the two girls now felt desperately sorry for both Mr and Mrs Robertson. However, though they felt sorry for their employers they still had no desire to stay with them and were both glad to be leaving.

The following week, two girls from the orphanage arrived. Daisy and Ethel showed them their jobs and then, in the evening, Daisy returned home for good. She took an affectionate farewell of Ethel and both girls agreed to write. As, however, the friendship had only really been based on need, each girl sent one letter to the other and that was the end of the friendship.

Nevertheless, despite the hard work, despite Mrs Robertson's general disagreeableness and the sense of unhappiness which pervaded the household, Daisy felt she had learnt quite a lot. She certainly now knew how to set an elegant table, though she felt she would not have much use for that knowledge in the Coffee House. She also had a better idea of how people in other walks of life lived and realised that possessions did not necessarily make for happiness. Nevertheless she could not help wishing that her mother owned some of the beautiful silver she had polished with so much pleasure in her employers' household, although she could not imagine where it could be put or when it could be used in the Coffee House.

Daisy was so glad to be back with her mother again that some of the bitterness in her heart at failing to be accepted for teacher training evaporated. She decided she would help her mother to the best of her ability and that between them they could perhaps make a success of the Coffee House. There was no doubt that her mother desperately needed more help and, loving her as she did, Daisy was prepared to be that help.

5
The Passing Years

One afternoon in the middle of February 1897, Lily came running home from school with the very unwelcome news that Gladys, one of the children in her class, was ill with diphtheria. Hannah looked up with a worried expression and asked whether the sick child sat near Lily in class and was glad to learn that Lily sat on the opposite side of the room. However Lily was rightly very afraid of diphtheria and remembered that, before she was born, her brother Ernest had died of the disease. Hannah tried to put Lily's mind at rest by saying that Ernest had been a sickly child and very young at the time, and that she was sure that Gladys would be all right. But Hannah was very far from sure that Gladys would be all right.

Diphtheria was a greatly feared disease – often a killer in those days. Hannah had lost one child to it and the fear of losing another filled her heart with dread. It was only two years since Esther had died and that wound was not and never would be truly healed. However, she did not wish to infect Lily with her fear, and changed the subject. Rhoda came in a little later. She had heard about Lily's classmate having the illness but then there was quite often an occasional case of the disease. Nothing more was said on the subject that day.

Two days later it was Rhoda who came home with news of the scourge. Two girls in the class below hers had caught it. Rhoda said that some children were staying away from school because their parents were afraid.

Hannah now became rather alarmed. She did not want Rhoda or Lily to be infected and wondered whether she should keep them at home. However neither girl wanted to stay at home; they preferred to go to school.

Six days later the news was very bad indeed. By now eight children were ill. The School Managers had been contacted and had ordered the drains to be checked. This had been done but they were found to be free from infection. Many parents were now keeping their children at home, unwilling to risk them catching the disease but still, each day, Lily and Rhoda insisted on going to school and each day, reluctantly, Hannah let them go.

Finally, when 10 children had caught the disease, the headmistress decided that the school must be closed. It was a decision forced on her by the parents, for the classrooms were now so empty that it was just not worthwhile keeping the school open. Miss Clutton, the Headmistress, contacted the Managers, who reluctantly agreed with her decision, though they were afraid that this might mean a reduction in the grant from the education authorities.

Rhoda and Lily, therefore, had an enforced holiday. Rhoda, now 13, loved school, mainly because she loved studying, and to Lily it was a refuge from the tyranny of her father.

Hannah, however, was grateful for the closure of the school. It hurt her to feel that her younger children preferred to be away from home, but she knew her husband's bad temper and sullen disposition frightened her youngest daughter and she understood Rhoda's thirst for knowledge.

As Rhoda was now old enough to be of assistance in the shop, Hannah took the opportunity of using her daughter's stay at home to give Daisy a few days' freedom and suggested she take Lily up to London to visit Aunt Susannah. Both girls were delighted with the idea. Lily particularly liked to visit London but there was rarely anyone with the time or money to spare to take her. She wished very much that she could travel up to town each day to work, as did her brother, David. Daisy pointed out that if Lily had to do it each day she would soon get tired of the travelling. Both girls enjoyed their expedition and their aunt was delighted to see them. They returned home to tell their mother of all the sights they had seen and hoped they would have another opportunity to visit Aunt Susannah fairly soon.

At the end of a fortnight, to the great delight of Rhoda and Lily, the school was reopened. However, a rule was passed by the Managers that no child must drink from the tap in the playground. It was thought possible that the germs had been passed from child to child through the use of the metal drinking mugs. There were now nearly 600 children in the school and none of them would be able to have a drink during school hours, however far they had come, however thirsty they might be.

The School Managers were still worried that diphtheria would recur. They were afraid that the children who had contracted the disease and recovered might come back too soon and the epidemic restart. In the end it was decided that all those who had caught diphtheria should have their throats checked and swabs taken before being allowed back to school. The cost of this scheme would be two shillings per child and, though the

Managers complained at this, it was found in the end to be a worthwhile expense. One child who had had the disease and wanted to come back to school was found to have a positive swab on two occasions. Had she returned without the check being made, the epidemic might well have restarted. When the Managers learnt of this case they became afraid lest a child who had the disease might move into the area and attend school while still carrying the infection. In order to avoid such a case, a rule was made that any new child who had had diphtheria and wanted admission to the school must have a negative swab before being allowed to start.

Hannah learnt later that three of the children who had caught the infection had died and that the others, though recovered, had been seriously debilitated by the disease. She was grateful that, on this occasion, tragedy had passed her family by.

When the two younger sisters returned to school after their unwanted holiday it was to find an innovation in the curriculum. This at first did not affect Lily as she was too young, but the girls in the two top classes were to be taught laundering. The School Managers, in their wisdom, had decided that all girls should learn this important subject and while the school was closed, wash boilers and other necessary equipment had been purchased and installed.

The laundry lesson was to take place immediately after the cookery class so that any used linen could be washed along with soiled articles which the girls had brought from home.

Rhoda was not over-enthusiastic at the thought of this new lesson, but as was her wont, she followed her teacher's instructions meticulously and brought back home articles in pristine condition for her mother to admire.

However, when Lily started laundry classes things did not work out so well. On the day of the lesson she would go to her mother and ask for some soiled article to take to school. Now Hannah did not like the thought of her family's dirty clothes being washed in public, so she would send her daughter with some article that to begin with was barely, if at all, dirty. Lily would work on this in the laundry lesson and then, of course, bring it home again. That was where the problem lay. Whatever Lily took to school to wash arrived home dirtier than when it had left the house. Poor Lily did not like it when Daisy picked up the object and went into peals of laughter at the state it was in, telling her sister that it was much dirtier than when her mother had given it to her and asking whether it had been washed in mud. Lily would run to Hannah for support and she would rebuke Daisy for being unkind. Lily learnt to smuggle the articles out and into the house so that her sister would not inspect and criticise her work.

That year turned out to be quite an eventful one. In May, Rhoda had a success. In school it had been suggested that the children should enter an RSPCA competition. They would have to write a story about an animal. Rhoda thought long and earnestly about this. Should she write a story about

34

a cat, a dog, or maybe a horse? In the end, passing by a cottage with a bedraggled canary sitting unhappily in its small cage and, at the same time hearing the cheerful song of a blackbird on a tree opposite, she wrote a pathetic story, imagining herself a caged canary, and making a plea, if not for freedom, at least for a cage large enough for her to stretch her wings and flutter around. She won. To her great delight she came out top in the competition and received both a certificate and a prize. The school was very proud of her and her success was reported to the Managers and entered in their records.

However, Rhoda's success was a very minor event compared with the Diamond Jubilee of 1897. Queen Victoria had reigned for 60 glorious years. Most of the people alive had not lived under any other monarch. She had a great Empire and the country was proud of her. Woodford was proud of her and plans were put in hand to make the event both patriotic and memorable.

First in importance, for future as well as present generations, was the Jubilee Hospital project. This was started by Mr Roberts, the owner of the then locally famous Roberts department store in Stratford, East London, who donated, at first anonymously, the sum of £2,000, the remainder of the money to be raised by the other inhabitants of Woodford.

Though the Cottage Hospital was to be the major project, a project lasting for posterity, Jubilee celebrations were also planned to take place on 21 June. The official day of the Jubilee was 22 June, but it was felt that, as Woodford was so near London, people might want to watch the celebrations there rather than remain in the village on that day.

Rhoda and Lily had been chattering about the arrangements for days and when 21 June arrived were in a state of great excitement. The celebrations were to start in the afternoon and, in the morning, with the exception of prayers for 'Our Queen, Country and Empire', school was to be as usual, or as near to usual as excited children could manage.

When the bell rang to release the children at midday, each of the teachers heaved a sigh of relief. Excited children are difficult to deal with and no one wished to be bad-tempered on that day.

Rhoda and Lily rushed back home for a light lunch. They knew a splendid tea was being provided and wanted to leave ample room for it. By 1.30 p.m. they were back at school.

The children were lined up in the playground in their classes and by the time they were all in their correct places they could hear the sound of music coming towards them. The children from Churchfields School in South Woodford had marched the considerable distance up the long incline of Salway Hill to Woodford Green, behind the Woodford Military Band, the Boys' Brigade and the Fire Brigade. When the procession had reached the School on the Green, the gates were opened and out came Rhoda and Lily and all the other children, bubbling with excitement but resolutely staying in their correct places. The children from the Green School joined the end of the procession and then all marched off to the stirring sounds of the military band.

Daisy had now left school for two years and would not be joining in the children's celebrations. She felt rather envious of Rhoda and Lily. Hannah suggested she might like to go up to the school and see the procession start, so, when she heard the sound of music, Daisy hurried to the school and wriggled her way through the crowd of parents gathered to watch their offspring march off.

As Daisy watched the procession start on its way to the Monkhams Estate, where food and entertainments had been arranged, she heard the sound of cheers, and brakes arrived bringing children from the Woodford Bridge School. Woodford Bridge is quite a considerable distance from Woodford Green and the children would not have been able to walk all the way to Monkhams from their school. The Woodford Bridge children scrambled down as quickly as possible and, again in classes, marched at the end of the procession. Following behind came the brakes, in which the children from Woodford Bridge and those too small to walk, would return after the celebrations.

Altogether 1,800 children, all waving Union Jacks, marched bravely along to the National Anthem and martial music. It normally took about a quarter of an hour to walk from the green to Monkhams Estate but, on this occasion, with so many children, it took much longer, and by the time the children reached their destination they were ready for refreshments.

The Vicar of All Saints had provided a magnificent tea for the children. It was set out on long trestle tables in the grounds of the estate. After tea the children ran races and played games and the winners were presented with prizes, again supplied by the Vicar. Finally the children gave three rousing cheers each for The Queen, 'God bless her', the Reverend Fitzpatrick, and, finally, for Mr Arnold Hills, the owner of Monkhams.

At 5.30 the children gathered again in their classes and those from Woodford Bridge, together with some of the weaker and smaller children from other schools, climbed into the brakes to be driven off in style, while the rest of the children had to march back the way they had come. This time they marched less smartly, feet dragged, children stumbled. They were all very weary and the Union Jacks still clutched in hot hands looked dirty and bedraggled. But though they arrived back home crotchety and tired, they had all enjoyed their afternoon.

At 9 o'clock that same evening, Monkhams was again open for visitors. 5,000 tickets had been issued to members of the Woodford community. Quite a lot of resentment and ill-feeling was caused on this occasion. Those who had not received tickets resented their exclusion from the evening's entertainment and some tried to creep in without being seen and when this failed made a commotion and were forcibly ejected.

36

Alfred had acquired two tickets for the entertainment but was not feeling very well that day and decided to stay at home. Hannah very much wanted to go. She had heard so much about the estate. As by 9 o'clock the younger children would be safely in bed, it was arranged that Hannah and Daisy should use the tickets. Hannah had felt sorry that Daisy had missed the day's celebrations, but Daisy was thrilled at the thought of going to the evening's entertainment.

At a quarter to nine mother and daughter joined the crowds walking towards Monkhams and long before they reached the estate could hear the bands playing in the grounds. Mr Hills, the owner, had arranged a display of fountains for his thousands of guests, but the novelty of these fountains was that they were lit by electric light. This was indeed an innovation. Gaslight was commonplace; electric light was not. It made the fountains look beautiful: the colours changed from yellow to red, red to green, green to blue. Hannah and Daisy gazed in wonder. Would they one day have electric light in their Coffee House? The idea seemed remote and unlikely, but to people 40 years or so earlier, when the only lighting after dark was by candles or lamps, perhaps gas would have seemed just as unlikely.

They returned home at about 11 p.m. and found that Alfred and David had festooned the Coffee House with red, white and blue streamers and hung out a large Union Jack from the parlour window. In the morning all the cottages around had red, white and blue on their windows and doors, while the shops in the main road were so patriotically decorated that it was hard to see what goods they were selling. There was no doubt of the patriotism of Woodford. The villagers were proud of their Queen and Empress, and they were proud to be British.

The next event in that year affecting the family was the flower show held in July. Perhaps the horses had been particularly productive that year, or perhaps Alfred had worked a little harder than usual on his allotment, or maybe he was just lucky. He had entered nearly all the classes in the cottage gardens section, and came first in most of them. In the section for the best kept allotment he had come second. He was extremely proud of his successes. When he returned to the shop he pinned his rosettes on the wall and was only too willing to explain to the customers how he had come by them.

Rhoda had entered a bunch of selected wild flowers and two buttonholes. In her case she achieved a third for her entries and was a little disappointed. She was sure her efforts were the best and did not agree with the judges at all.

Hannah had wondered what she could enter and looking down the various classes she noticed one for a selection of cooked vegetables. Though so busy in the shop and home she still managed to find time to select the best of Alfred's vegetables, prepare them carefully and cook them to perfection. For her trouble she received a second prize.

At the end of the month, Rhoda finished her elementary schooling. She

37

had, like Daisy before her, stayed for an additional year and helped with the younger children, but, unlike Daisy, she was accepted as a pupil teacher. She had proved to be one of the brightest girls the school had produced, and the authorities were prepared to support her application.

However, she had to obtain her father's permission. He had to sign her indentures. Unfortunately he did not approve of girls having careers, especially his girls. They were brought into the world to pander to his whims and perhaps later, the whims of their husbands. He expected them to be his obedient servants and he did not want to sign away his authority. Pupil teaching meant that Rhoda would have more education and would perhaps consider herself better informed than others, better informed than her father.

Alfred's health was now very bad. His heart was gradually deteriorating and he was suffering from dropsy. Periodically he had to go into hospital to have excess water removed and it was after he had come home from a stay in hospital that the indenture form was received by Rhoda. Her mother took it to Alfred and told him that it was an important document on which the authorities needed his signature. She was very vague about its purpose and he, without enquiring too deeply, signed. Immediately afterwards Rhoda put it in an envelope and ran off to post it. Alfred realising that he had not really enquired into what he was signing, questioned Hannah more closely about the document. Since the form had been posted and there was no further need to hide the truth, she explained that it was Rhoda's indentures and that she could now become a pupil teacher. He was furious, especially when he realised that he should have read it through and that he had been duped, but there was now nothing he could do.

Rhoda had started on the road that would lead her to becoming a qualified teacher. In her case, unlike Daisy's, it was not the desire to teach that spurred her, but a thirst for knowledge. The only way she could obtain further education was by attending the local pupil teachers' centre. The education at this centre was somewhat similar to that at a grammar school and she would be able to take various public examinations and, if she did well enough, might gain admission to a college where she would be able to study for her Teacher's Certificate.

The local centre which Rhoda had to attend was in Churchfields School. This had only recently been opened. Previously pupil teachers had to travel to a London centre, but expenses had to be cut and the authorities thought it would cost less to provide a local centre for the pupils to attend than to send them outside the area. This, however, did not prove to be the case, as the expense of the Churchfields centre was greater than anticipated. Although there were rumblings of discontent at this expense and demands that the centre be closed, it continued to operate.

At the end of Rhoda's first year at the centre, when the students took their yearly exams, she came out top. The School on the Green and her family, except perhaps her father, were all very proud of her, none more so than Daisy who could see her younger sister fulfilling her own ambition. She may have been a little jealous of Rhoda's success but didn't show it. However, it became obvious as time went on that, instead of Rhoda looking to Daisy for advice, it was Daisy who now looked up to Rhoda and this rather sapped her confidence in herself.

When Daisy was 17 a breach occurred in the family which never really healed. Daisy had developed into an attractive lively young woman and was now, of course, constantly coming into contact with the customers in the shop. Hannah would try and reserve to herself those customers whose conversation was 'smutty' and whose manners were unpleasantly rough and who delighted in embarrassing the young girl. There were, however, many other customers of whom Hannah approved and these the girl would serve and with them she became popular. One particular customer used to come in time and time again. His name was John Collins. He used to engage Daisy in conversation and was obviously attracted to her. After a while he asked her to go for a walk with him. As her parents seemed to approve, she went out with him and she enjoyed being escorted by such a good looking man. It soon became obvious that Collins was courting Daisy and Daisy was undeniably flattered. She was not sure what her own feelings were but her heart certainly fluttered whenever he came into the shop and she used to blush becomingly. She sometimes thought about marriage, but she was not at all sure she would like to leave her home and spend her life with Collins. She was not sure she was ready for such a move. Collins asked Alfred whether he would object if he asked Daisy to be his wife. Alfred certainly did object. He liked Collins but told him that Daisy was too young and he would not give his permission for a year or two. Collins accepted the decision and so matters remained for a while.

Ada, who had been away in service, now returned home for a short stay and Collins happened to come along to the shop, hoping to see Daisy, while Ada was there. Ada was rather like Daisy in appearance, though she had a gentler, quieter disposition. She was also older than Daisy and quite anxious to get married.

Collins noticed the similarity between the two sisters and having been rebuffed, turned his attentions to Ada, much to Daisy's amazement and chagrin. Ada, as Daisy had been, was flattered. The rest of the family were appalled. Hannah tried to reason with Ada, but the girl had become infatuated. She was now over 21; many of her schoolfriends had married and she, too, wanted a home of her own. Despite the rest of the family's disapproval of his behaviour, Collins could not very well be stopped from using the coffee shop. Although Hannah made it plain that she objected to his attentions to her eldest daughter, Ada quite obviously enjoyed them and preferred to ignore the fact that she had stolen her sister's admirer.

39

Daisy by now would not speak to Ada, so hurt was she by her sister's behaviour. At night she would pummel the pillow with anger and then, burying her face in it sob with distress. Rhoda tried to comfort her and the two drew even closer. It was not that Daisy really wanted to marry Collins – she would not have him now if he asked her on bended knees – but her pride was desperately hurt. That her eldest sister had caused this hurt was beyond her comprehension. Did she not have any loyalty or consideration for her family? She knew Collins had asked her, Daisy, to marry him, why then had Ada encouraged him? Daisy valued loyalty herself and the actions of her sister were completely alien to her.

Apart from the fact that Collins was very good looking and that she had become infatuated with him, another reason for Ada's defection might well have been her father's attitude to the man. Although Hannah disliked him, her husband did not, and on many occasions played chess with him in the shop. Alfred had not wanted Daisy to marry because it would have interfered with his comfort. Ada had not been at home so much and it would not make much difference to his life if she married. Ada was afraid of her father and did not like living in the same house with him. Marriage to Collins opened up a way of escape which would not merit her father's disapproval. Alfred's temper was greatly feared by them all and his ill-humour would permeate everything, it was like a cold wet blanket that kept out warmth and love.

In the end, despite opposition from Hannah and the obvious disapproval of Ada's siblings, Collins married Ada. Daisy, of course, refused to have anything to do with the marriage. She did not want to go to it or hear about it. She would look after the shop; somebody had to. No one argued with her and, when Ada and Collins returned to the shop after the wedding, Daisy went straight out and did not return until the newlyweds had left.

Ada's marriage was not happy. In many ways Daisy had, at that time, a stronger character than her sister. She would stand up for what she thought was right. Ada, on the other hand was so infatuated with her husband that she was prepared to be subservient to him and he took advantage of this and privately despised her for it. He was at times quite brutal so that, finally, Ada applied for a separation order, which was granted. She was, however, still infatuated with her husband and could not stay away and the order was revoked. Daisy by this time was on speaking terms with her sister, but though prepared to help her if necessary, had not forgotten nor forgiven.

Unfortunately, Ada was also aware that her husband still found Daisy attractive. Watching her playing the piano he would express admiration of Daisy's hands and her cleverness at the piano. Daisy, however, no longer found Ada's husband at all attractive and, although she would never have admitted it to Ada, was glad that her eldest sister was the one John Collins had married.

After their marriage the couple ran a bicycle shop in London and Ada had children in rapid succession. Her second pregnancy resulted in twins, a sickly pair, who died in infancy. The twins were followed by a son and then, after the legal separation was annulled, she produced two more daughters. The bicycle shop did not prove very profitable and Ada had a struggle to feed her family. Then, while her two youngest children were little more than infants, John Collins developed cancer and Ada had to cope with a very sick husband, a large family and the shop. It was a hand to mouth existence. Her husband finally died while still a relatively young man and Ada had to struggle on. When, finally, Daisy married and left the Coffee House, Ada and her family moved in to help Hannah.

Even after John Collins had died, Daisy could not really forgive her sister for what she considered her treachery. If Ada ever needed help Daisy would come to her assistance; but she would never show affection. The older sister tried hard to heal the breach and when Daisy married and had children, those children became very fond of their aunt, who was unfailingly kind. But Daisy never forgot. She did not tell her own children of the incident until they were married themselves, and when young, they did not understand why their mother was not so friendly with Auntie Ada as with Aunties Rhoda and Lily.

It was a pity that Daisy was unable to forgive and forget. After all, Ada had suffered while Daisy herself had a relatively happy marriage. Perhaps Daisy would have found more peace of mind if she could have put the whole thing behind her – but she could not.

As Alfred became older and sicker so he became more and more difficult to live with. He continually criticised his wife and found fault with the girls. On one occasion it all became too much for long-suffering Hannah, who put on her bonnet and coat and walked out of the shop saying as she did so that she had no intention of returning and that, if he was always going to criticise, he could run things by himself.

Alfred was considerably shaken as his wife walked away from the shop. He did not really believe that she would carry out her threat. After all where could she go? What could she do? But he was not sure. He knew that Hannah was at times a very determined woman, but surely she would not leave Lily and Aubrey, and what about the shop, who could manage that? After a few minutes he turned to Daisy, who had watched horrified, and said to her 'You and I will manage together quite well without your mother'. Daisy looked at him disgustedly and retorted that if her mother went she would go to. She added that she had no intention of running the Coffee House with him as he didn't know how to treat anyone decently; and then turning on her heel she marched out of the room. Her father had never had such a rebellion before. He put the 'Closed' notice on the door and waited for the remaining customers, who had watched the scene with interest, to depart. He wondered what he should do. Would he be able to manage? Did his wife truly mean to leave him for good? He couldn't really believe that she would leave her children whom she loved so much. But he just was not sure. There was a chance she might not return. In despair he was wondering what to do and how he could possibly manage when, to his great delight, Hannah returned. He had never been more pleased to see her in his life. Unfortunately the incident was of no lasting benefit and he was soon as bad-tempered as ever.

All Daisy's life, she had looked up to her brother David. She adored him. He was her playmate and instructor, her ideal of what a boy and later a young man should be. He left school when he was 13 and worked as an office boy in the City. He was a reserved youth and did not often mix with the customers in the Coffee House. In fact he preferred to keep out of the shop altogether if he could. He was not particularly liked by the clientele to whom, if he met them, he was always very pleasant, but who considered him rather 'stuck up'. Occasionally he might play a game of chess with someone he liked but usually he kept aloof.

Although he had been forced to leave school as soon as possible by his father, he was a clever lad and ambitious. He wanted to go into the Post Office as a clerk and work his way up. This would give him a secure future and one he thought he would enjoy. However, to achieve this ambition he had to pass an examination and he had only received the minimum elementary education available. He bought as many books as he could afford, and, after work each evening, studied hard. Despite the fact that he was employed during the day and worked hard each evening, he was still very much under the domination of his father who expected him, when necessary, to help keep the allotment going and, if this could not be done at any other time, it had to be in the evening, whatever else David had intended to do.

At last the day of the examination came. David sat and a week or so later learned that he had passed and passed well. He was overjoyed and excited. His future was secure, he would always have a job and would be able to work his way up. Life lay rosily ahead. He would be able to marry and support a wife, there was one girl he liked a great deal. Who knew what might happen? Then the blow struck. Before being finally accepted by the postal authorities he had to have a medical examination by his local doctor one evening after his return from work.

On that particular evening as he entered the Coffee House he was greeted by his father with the news that there was a load of manure which David must take down to the allotment. The youth was horrified and explained to his father that he had got to have his medical examination that evening. His father roughly replied he didn't care about that but if his son hurried he could carry out both tasks. David was appalled. It was a long way to trundle the barrow on the best of occasions, but to do it at speed and then rush to the doctor's afterwards, he could not believe that his father meant it.

42

Unfortunately Alfred did mean it. Despite being the oldest son, David was not a favourite of his father. They had nothing in common. Hannah tried to intercede but to no avail. Alfred simply shouted at her, accusing her of spoiling her son. Alfred expected his children to obey him and the habit of obedience was too strong for David. He changed into his old clothes, took the loaded barrow and trundled it as quickly as he could to the allotment. He reloaded it with produce and hurried back as fast as possible up the long hill. He reached the Coffee House tired out. He had no time for a meal, that would have to wait. He changed into better clothes and rushed off to the doctor's. By the time he reached the surgery his heart was pounding and he felt very nervous.

The doctor examined him but would not pass him as fit. He said his heart was not behaving normally. In view of the rushing about David had done that evening, it is quite possible that the diagnosis was wrong, but in any case the job for which he was being examined was not a manual one and would not have required great physical strength. Nevertheless because the doctor would not pass him as fit, all the study had been in vain, his dream of a rosy future disappeared. He could not now enter the Post Office.

Hannah was quite sure that had David not had to cart the manure to the allotment that evening but had rested before going to the doctor's, he would have passed his medical. Whether or not this was true the fact remained that the rest of the family blamed David's failure at the medical examination on the harshness and lack of consideration shown by his father.

Alfred was thoroughly disliked by most of the members of his family. His wife would avoid him as much as she possibly could and the girls feared him. Daisy, however, if necessary, was prepared to stand up for what she thought was right but even so, for the sake of peace, would avoid confrontation as much as possible. The only family member for whom Alfred showed affection was Aubrey. Although David was the eldest son, his father's affection was showered on his youngest child. Aubrey was a lively intelligent toddler with a friendly disposition. Being the youngest, he expected and received a great deal of attention from the other members of the family, including his father.

As the last years of the nineteenth century rolled slowly on, life in the village seemingly went on at its accustomed pace. The flower shows attracted their usual number of exhibitors, Alfred among them, taking most of the prizes in the cottagers' classes. Daisy, her mother and sisters won prizes for cookery. On one occasion the prizes were new silver coins supplied by the manager of the Woodford branch of the Joint Stock Bank. These facts and many others were duly recorded in the local paper.

But times were changing. In May 1898, Gladstone, the Grand Old Man of the Liberal Party, died. Born in 1809, he had become an institution. Alfred was an enthusiastic Liberal and he was most upset at the death of Gladstone. Somehow, like the Queen, he had seemed indestructible. Alfred foretold the doom of the Liberal Party and deterioration in the condition of the common people now that the most famous member of the Liberal Party had died. He was not the only one who regretted Gladstone's death. The following Sunday throughout Woodford in all the churches, sermons were preached extolling the virtues and achievements of the Grand Old Man.

Gladstone's longevity was attributed by Hannah to the fact that every mouthful of food he had eaten had been masticated 30 times. How Hannah acquired this belief it is impossible to say, yet it was a firmly held one that was passed on to Daisy. She in her turn would tell her own children and grandchildren when they gulped down a meal too quickly, that if they wanted to live long healthy lives they, too, like Gladstone, must chew every mouthful 30 times. Mockers of later generations would greet this statement with the unbelieving comment: 'How did he manage with rice pudding and jelly?'

Another change that affected members of the community was that emigration to Canada was being encouraged. Free land grants of 160 acres were offered to enterprising emigrants. Daisy lost a friend from church this way. He took up the challenge and he and his young family emigrated to start a new life in Canada.

The Green School still remained of great importance to Rhoda and Lily and news of it interested the rest of the family. One day Rhoda came home with the information that the school was getting a new assistant teacher, and added that it was not before time as the number of children had increased so greatly. When asked if she had seen the new teacher Rhoda replied that she had and that she had been introduced to her as the pupil teacher. Rhoda also added that the new teacher seemed very pleasant. She then told her mother that she had learnt from the other teachers that someone else had been the first choice of the Managers, but had turned down the position because she was offered another job nearer London where she would receive £55 a year instead of the £50 offered by the Green School.

When Rhoda returned home the next day, she came with the news that the teacher just appointed had also decided not to accept. She, too, had been offered a post with more money elsewhere. Rhoda was indignant. To her £50 sounded a vast sum but Hannah was more practical. She knew the value of money and £5 more a year was quite a consideration to someone living on her own. Finally, the Managers of the School decided that they would fall into line with other schools and offer more money and the post was readvertised at a higher rate. Rhoda wished she were qualified and could apply.

There were other problems at the School. One lunch-time Lily came home crying. She had not been able to find her coat. It was not on her peg and she had looked everywhere but she just could not find it. Hannah asked if Lily had reported the loss to her teacher but the child had come straight home and not told her teacher. Hannah told Lily she must tell her teacher directly she returned to school. Rumour had gone around the village that there had been cases of stealing at the school and Hannah was afraid that Lily had been a victim. This was indeed the case and as the coat was not found poor Lily was forced to wear a very old one for the time being.

A week or so later the thieves were found. A boy and girl aged 13 and 11 from a squalid cottage near the Coffee House, had been stealing clothes and selling them to a pawnbroker. The children were brought up before the Magistrates at Stratford Court and were treated as first offenders and their parents reprimanded. The pawnbroker was also censured for accepting clothes from children. Although he pleaded that he did not know the clothes were stolen, because the mother had previously sent the children with similar goods to pawn, he was ordered to return the stolen property to its rightful owners and to refrain from accepting anything from children in future. When Hannah learned who the culprits were she was sorry. She knew their mother, a woman with a useless drunken husband, fighting against the odds to keep herself and her family respectable. Lily's coat was returned but she never liked wearing it afterwards.

Another problem that hit the Green School in the summer of 1898 was an outbreak of measles. Half of the infants caught the disease. Hannah was very grateful that Aubrey had not yet started his schooling and watched anxiously for signs of the disease. He was at this time an ailing child and six months later the doctor would issue his ultimatum, a year in bed or else an early death. But at this time the little boy was still allowed his freedom. Lily had had measles when she was tiny so there was no question of her bringing the infection home. Hannah was nevertheless very glad when the epidemic abated. After losing two of her children she had become very protective of the others. Though measles could be dangerous, especially for a weak and undernourished child, it was not so deadly as diphtheria and the school remained open throughout the epidemic.

The privilege of having Epping Forest on its doorstep also brought problems to the village. The forest, then as now, was very much the playground of East London. The East Enders came out determined both to enjoy themselves in the fresh air and to wake up the rustic inhabitants of Woodford. As the brakes rattled noisily through the village, large lighted coloured matches were thrown at the passers-by. There were many complaints about this behaviour and once as Lily was pushing Aubrey along in his pushchair a flaring coloured match was thrown at them but just missed. Lily was frightened, but Aubrey excited.

However, no one was very pleased at the next incident when one of these matches actually landed on a passer-by, setting fire to her dress, a fire quickly extinguished by those around. On this occasion the culprit was caught and convicted at Stratford Magistrates' Court and from then on that particular nuisance ceased.

There were other annoyances associated with the East London brakes. In the summer months they would clatter through Woodford regularly on Sunday mornings, taking trippers to the forest and when passing through the village the trippers would blow horns and make as much noise as possible. Sometimes the noise would interrupt a sermon exposing the wickedness of the world and sometimes Daisy, playing a gentle hymn tune in the little chapel, would find the noise of the horns distracted her, causing her fingers to play a discord. Many complaints were made, but the annoyance continued. The Free Church was forced to move to the Green.

In June 1899 the Jubilee Hospital was opened. It was only a small hospital but was of importance to Hannah and her family, and it was to this hospital that Alfred now went when he needed special nursing, and it was there that Lily had her tonsils humanely removed.

In October of that year the second Boer War started and the local paper was full of sad news of casualties and of British refugees from the Transvaal, bereft of homes and possessions. Funds were promptly started by the churches to give assistance to the refugees and widows and orphans of soldiers and great concern was felt by everyone. The rights and wrongs of the war were heatedly discussed with, in some cases, sympathy being expressed for the Boers, but Kruger soon became an anathema.

6

A New Century Begins

The beginning of the new century was indeed a time of change for the family at the Coffee House. It was also an eventful time for the country as a whole. The Boer War was in progress; patriotism was well to the fore. Britain had her Empire, Queen Victoria was still on the throne, although now a very old woman, and the Boers were the enemy. But although they were the enemy they were proving exceptionally good fighters. They were fighting for their land and they believed their cause was just and that the British were the interlopers.

Feelings in Britain ran very high. All that could be done to help the gallant soldiers of the Queen should be done and Woodford would set an example. Jubilee Hospital's number of beds had been increased to 10, and one of these was offered to the War Office for the use of a wounded soldier. When Ladysmith was relieved there was great jubilation and, along with most of the other houses and cottages, the Coffee House hung out its large

Union Jack. Later, Lily running in from school asked her mother for a penny for the soldiers. She told Hannah that the school was having a collection for those who had been hurt in the fighting. Alfred grunted to the effect that they were always being asked for money but even he had fallen prey to the mounting patriotism and Lily received her penny. The school was able to send the grand sum of £4 10s 8d. It sounds a small amount now but it represented a definite sacrifice for some of the community.

Young Aubrey, now, once more, allowed his mobility to the relief of his family, ran round the shop shooting at everyone with a pretend gun. He was a brave British soldier killing all the bad Boers. He even shot his father, who managed a sour smile for his favourite child and shot back on behalf of the Boers.

The needlework lessons at school were used for making useful articles for the soldiers and 150 items were sent out to South Africa. Lily found it even more tedious to knit socks for soldiers than the smaller ones needed for her little brother. However, as a relief from the boredom of sock knitting, she decided to enter a dressed doll in the Woodford Exhibition of Industry and Art. Lily was not the only one to exhibit at this show. Daisy was not a good dressmaker, she did not like needlework, and in future years when she made clothes for her own children it was out of necessity only. She was, however, a very good plain cook and decided to enter six jam tarts and a potato pie; her mother, not to be outdone, felt that she could manage to make half a pint of barley water.

All these items were duly submitted and to their amazement each gained first prize in her section. Lily was extremely proud of her doll and sat it in a prominent place in the shop until roughly told to move it by her irascible father.

There had been much talk, in the Congregational Church Hannah and the family attended, of another church of the same denomination which was to be built in the Ray Lodge area of Woodford, nearer the River Roding. Collections had been made to gather funds for the proposed church and now the building was about to begin. In May there was to be the stone-laying ceremony and Hannah was determined to go. As the event was to be in the evening she decided to shut the shop early and Daisy said she would go along with her mother. In fact, although at the time Daisy did not realise it, the Church at Ray Lodge was to have a profound effect on her life, leading to her eventual marriage with Richard, the boy who, many years earlier, had watched the lively young girl through the school railings.

There had been a mission hall at Ray Lodge for many years but London was spreading its boundaries. Woodford was growing rapidly and the village was beginning to become a suburb. With the increase in population and in the attendance at the mission hall, it had become necessary to build a larger Congregational Church to replace the hall.

The important people on this occasion were the Spicer family whose home was Harts, a large house set back from the Green. Many years later it was to become a hospital. This family had been connected with the area for many years and were very philanthropic, deeply involved with the Congregational movement. Evan Spicer made a speech which greatly interested Hannah and her daughter. He said how 30 years previously there had been two black spots in Woodford. One was the area at the back of the Castle, the area in fact where the Coffee House was situated, and the other Ray Lodge. Evan Spicer went on to say that now the Castle area was being sought after by wealthy people because of the delightful views it offered across Epping Forest, with, in the right weather, truly wonderful sunsets. Hannah realised how true this was. She too, in her occasional free time, enjoyed walking along the road by the school and had sometimes gazed entranced as the setting sun changed the forest into a place of great beauty.

During the time Hannah had been living at the Coffee House, many fine houses had been built along Sunset Avenue which ran along by the side of the Green School. Although behind the Castle itself there were still many somewhat small and squalid cottages, the area generally had changed and was still changing. There was talk of the Highams Estate being broken up which would alter Woodford still more. Hannah did not like the thought of that. Evan Spicer ended his talk by saying that the Ray Lodge district had now also become respectable as was evidenced by the desire for a larger Congregational Church.

In one way and another the Spicer family played an important part in Daisy's fortunes and those of her sister Rhoda. In Rhoda's case it was with the help of Miss Spicer that she was able to go to Homerton College, Cambridge. For Daisy the help was more indirect. It was through the Spicer family that her husband, Richard, found his employment. At the turn of the century in Woodford, the Spicer sisters were well known and respected. Inhibited by their sex from taking an active part in politics (one of the Spicer sisters once said at a Liberal meeting that being a woman meant you had no vote and were nothing) they turned their intelligence and interest to helping the local community in the best way they could.

A few days after the stone-laying ceremony a national event occurred. Mafeking was relieved. Daisy had gone to bed rather late the night before and at about 5.30 a.m. the next morning she was suddenly woken up by loud shouting. Rhoda next to her stirred, wondering what was happening. The two sisters got out of bed. It was very early and they could not imagine why there was so much shouting in the road below.

The girls looked through the little window and could see people shouting and cheering. They dressed hurriedly and went down into the square. Rhoda saw a neighbour they knew well and asked what had happened. She was told that the early carts out from London had brought the wonderful news that Mafeking had been relieved.

Daisy and Rhoda ran back into the Coffee House. They decided to hang

48

out the big Union Jack which was kept for special national occasions. Together they hung it from the parlour window and noticed that many other flags were appearing in the cottages around.

That day was busier than usual. Excited customers stayed longer to chat about the news and from all sides Kruger and the Boers were vilified. By the time evening had come Woodford had organised itself for a celebration, a bonfire on the green. Lily came home from school with the news that someone had made an effigy of Kruger and it was going to be burnt on the bonfire that evening.

Hannah decided that she and the family would go over and watch, after the Coffee House was shut. At 9 o'clock the family trooped out leaving Aubrey safely asleep and Alfred dozing in the parlour.

However, when Hannah and her family reached the green their pleasure in the occasion quickly turned to disgust. The effigy had not yet been burnt but some louts had got hold of it and with a viciousness which shocked and horrified the family, were beating it with sticks and calling it obscene names. Hannah asked the girls whether they would like to return home but, although disgusted, they decided they would like to see the bonfire. When the bonfire was blazing fiercely, the louts, with a final yell of execration, hurled Kruger's effigy into the flames. As that happened Hannah turned on her heels and walked back to her home followed by her children. She was disgusted with what she had seen. Her pleasure in the relief of Mafeking was quenched by the viciousness she had seen displayed around her and she began to wonder what exactly the war was about and who the Boers really were and why they fought so bravely. She really did not know the rights and wrongs of their case. These thoughts, however, though briefly mentioned to Daisy and Rhoda, were mainly kept to herself.

Her neighbours would have considered her extremely unpatriotic if she had expressed doubts about the rightness of the war. She learnt later, though, that many of her friends and neighbours, especially those from the church, were as disgusted as she had been by the behaviour at the bonfire.

On 28 May 1900, a Thursday, the children were granted a whole day's holiday, half of the day was for the Queen's birthday and the other half for the relief of Mafeking. In the afternoon there was to be a great carnival to raise money for the Essex War Fund, and the whole village turned out. Hannah, not feeling so enthusiastic now about the Mafeking celebrations, said she would stay behind and look after the shop, which was not busy anyway, and the others could watch the carnival. Daisy and her two sisters, with Aubrey firmly held between them, managed to get in a good position on the roadside to admire the floats as they came by. But long before these came in sight, the sound of the local bands assailed their ears, nearer and nearer came the bands and louder and louder came the music. The bands were headed, as usual, by the Woodford Military Band and all of the members were blowing their cheeks out as they rendered the stirring strains of

'Soldiers of the Queen' to the cheers of the crowds. They did vary this with other martial tunes, but back came the favourite time and time again.

Following the bands came the floats to the 'Oohs' and 'Ahs' of the bystanders. Some of the floats were attractive, some funny but all were admired and the girls found it very hard to say which they preferred. It took two hours before the whole procession had passed, by which time the bystanders had begun to get very restive, especially little Aubrey.

The family returned home to tell their mother all about it, but when they reached the Coffee House they were greeted with a request from a very harassed Hannah to go and fetch the doctor quickly as father was ill again.

As the year had progressed so Alfred's health and temper had deteriorated. He became so crotchety and bad-tempered that his family kept out of his way as much as possible. He complained at any noise and even Aubrey, his favourite, was shouted at, though it was usually poor Lily who bore most of the brunt of his ill-humour and was thus denied a happy childhood. She was now 11 years of age and for as long as she could remember, her father had frightened and repressed her, although she, like all the others, loved her mother dearly.

Now, however, Alfred was really very ill and yet he would not give up his interest in his allotment. He still persevered with his gardening. It required great will power on his part to get to the allotment and still greater to get back home again up the long hill, especially if he was carrying anything, and by the time he reached home he would be in a state of collapse and sink exhausted into a chair. David, of course, was still expected to fetch and carry after work in the evenings. But it was Alfred who unwisely dug, planted and tended his vegetables and fruit as he had always done. He apparently loved his allotment far more than his home, and his plants far more than his family. This year again, despite his ill-health, he entered about a dozen items for the horticultural show in July and again won prizes for them all – perhaps not so many firsts this time, but nevertheless a satisfactory number, and he was also awarded a special prize for his allotment.

At the end of July the weather turned very hot indeed and this worried Alfred. Indeed it worried others, too, and several in the area died of heat stroke. The weather exacerbated his heart condition. His breathing became very bad indeed and he was obviously in considerable pain. The doctor was called and ordered him into hospital immediately.

On 4 August he was still in the Jubilee Hospital and the weather remained hot and oppressive. However, he was allowed up and was sitting by the table in the middle of the ward playing a game of draughts with a fellow sufferer when he suddenly collapsed. By the time the nurse reached him he was dead.

When Alfred died he was still relatively young, being in his late forties. He had been in every respect a Victorian father, the ruler of his household and an autocrat but, unfortunately, in his latter years, a liability. None of the younger members of the family regretted his passing. No doubt Hannah remembering past years when he was still an active and attractive man, shed the odd tear. But life would now become easier for her. When young Lily, who was wiping down the tables in the shop, heard the news of her father's death in hospital her only comment was 'Thank God', which she meant most sincerely. During her childhood he had become steadily more and more difficult to live with and as his bouts of ill-health increased he had seemed to take a particular aversion to the young girl and her natural gaiety had to be suppressed. Indeed for many years there had been little cheer for the family in the Coffee House.

Even taking his ill-health into account it is still puzzling that a man should have gone out of his way to be so unpleasant and end up so unloved. He was, after all, very intelligent and had a variety of interests. Any work he did, any ideas he had, were competently carried out. He was a good chess player and was interested in the politics of the time, generally arguing from the Liberal standpoint. Although not helping in the running of the Coffee House itself, the produce from his allotment must have been a great help to the family's finances. He was, however, as has been said, a man of his times and in the Victorian period the father was in control of his children's lives with no consideration for their views.

After her husband's funeral, Hannah invited his relatives back to the Coffee House, closed on this occasion, for a 'cold collation'. This was Aunt Susannah's idea. As ever a bulwark in times of trouble, it was she who suggested and organised the meal. Daisy had never heard the expression 'cold collation' before and to her it became synonymous with funerals. Hannah, Aunt Susannah and Daisy prepared the food, which was, as usual, very good.

This meal was intended to be one of farewell not only to Alfred but to all his relatives. Hannah found herself in a difficult position. As Alfred's widow his relatives expected her to be unhappy and weep. Perhaps, in private she did weep a little for the man who had just died, for a marriage that way back in the past did have moments of pleasure and happiness, but which in later years had developed into a weary grind. His relatives gathered together and sang his praises, commenting among themselves on Hannah's hardness of heart. Alfred's offspring, realising what was expected of them, did their best to appear sad and subdued, but such an attitude was hard to sustain for they knew that no more would their father's sour face quench any gaiety.

Yet remembering the Christmases when Daisy was young, when Alfred's health was better and when he had really encouraged the family to enjoy themselves, perhaps if he had suffered less pain and had better health he might have been a kinder father and husband. Who can say? Maybe it is only right to give him the benefit of the doubt.

Hannah now saw no reason for continuing any contact with Alfred's relations and from this time onwards communication with them ceased. Daisy and her brothers and sisters therefore had very little knowledge of any of their paternal cousins.

7

Life after Death – the Coffee House without Alfred

Daisy was 19 when her father died. Ada, now aged 25, was of course married. David, 21, a personable young man, was working as a clerk in the City and Rhoda was established as a pupil teacher hoping eventually to go to college. Lily was still only a child of 11 and her young brother Aubrey a mischievous little boy of five. Until her father's death Lily had been subdued and dominated by his bad temper which lay like a dark cloud over the home. She was stopped from laughing and playing and told to keep quiet otherwise she would upset her father. She must have been a lonely child when not at school which she loved as a place of release. There were five years between her and her nearest sister, Rhoda, and Rhoda's companion, when at home, was definitely Daisy. Lily's friend in the home was Aubrey, six years her junior.

Eleven years of age in those days was considered nearly grown up. After all, Ada had left school at 12 and David at 13. However, Lily's childhood came after her father's death. Aubrey was given a pair of roller skates; Lily learnt to roller skate. Aubrey liked climbing trees, he was now fit enough to do so. Of course, Lily must climb trees, too. She and her little brother would cajole their mother into letting them take a snack up into the branches of an old oak that grew near Chingford Lane and, in their leafy refuge, they would watch unseen the activities of their friends and neighbours. David would come walking along with Olive. Mrs Robertson would pass near them dressed up in her best proudly stalking along on her way to pay a call on a friend and then, of course, there would be a fight between some of the big, rougher boys from the School on the Green.

Lily enjoyed all the freedom she had missed during the previous 11 years of her life, when repressed and subdued, she grew up loathing every aspect of the Coffee House. When in later years her niece asked about her life as a child she replied that she did not want to remember as she hated every aspect of it. However she did remember her escapades on the green with brother Aubrey and specifically mentioned the roller-skating and tree-climbing with food eaten in the hideout. Hannah must have watched with understanding her young daughter's loneliness and unhappiness over the years but she was much too busy and had too many problems of her own to be able to help Lily. She did her best to show how much she loved the child but was unable to make life easier for her as long as Alfred was alive.

Lily remembered the day of her father's death as being the happiest of her life so far. A great black cloud rolled away and the sun came out for Lily, and, for the next year or so, until she had to become a 'young lady', she ran free and played joyously with Aubrey on the green and in the forest near their home.

With Alfred's death, life became easier, not only for Lily but for all the others as well. Not only was there a more relaxed atmosphere, but there were no more hospital or doctor's bills to pay for him. He had never helped in the shop, so Hannah did not miss him there. With the relaxed atmosphere the shop began to prosper. There was more money around. The chickens were gradually disposed of and never replaced. No longer would the girls have to hawk the eggs round the neighbourhood. Of course the allotment also had to be abandoned by the family and though perhaps the lack of fresh home grown vegetables was regretted by Hannah and, maybe, the customers, David particularly was glad not to have to trundle the barrow down and up that long hill. He now had more time in which to meet his friends and he was becoming very interested in one of his young neighbours, Olive Carpenter.

Although Lily's childhood had become easier, there were many other children living around her for whom times were hard and who lived their lives in bitter, grinding poverty, such as she had not known. These children were often sent to school hungry, if, indeed, they were able to go to school at all, lacking, as so many of them did, sufficient clothing and shoes.

One cold January day Lily came in thoughtfully from school at lunchtime and asked her mother if there were any warm clothes of hers that she had outgrown and were of no more use. Her mother expressed surprise and Lily explained that her teacher had said that some of the children in the other classes could not go to school because their clothes and shoes were worn out. Hannah remembered a pair of boots that Lily had outgrown and suggested that the child take them as they were in fairly good condition. She then suggested that Lily should look in her chest of drawers to see if there were other articles she no longer needed. Lily came downstairs with a selection of clothing, some of which Hannah allowed her to take back to school.

Around the square in which the Coffee House stood were, at that time, streets of small cottages. Most of the inmates of these cottages, though not having a comfortable income were, nevertheless, able to sustain a fair standard of living. There were others, however, who found this impossible.

There were families where sickness had robbed the breadwinner of his income and where, perhaps, the mother was endeavouring to support her family on her meagre wages as a washerwoman. Hannah had the assistance of one of these women, aged about 35 but haggard and worn, looking about double her age. Knowing how hard the woman had to struggle to make ends meet, Hannah would augment the money she paid with food from the shop. There were, of course, other families where the parents thoughtlessly drank away what little money they were able to obtain and whose children had an impossible existence. Whatever the reason, there were many children, that cold winter, who were unable to attend school because they had insufficient clothing.

The teachers at the Green School aware that the children who had the greatest need to be at school were the ones least able to attend, had started a clothing pool from which they were able to give a little help to some of the poorest children.

It was a cold and comfortless time that winter and became even more comfortless when suddenly on 22 January the death of Queen Victoria shocked the nation. Hannah and her family had never known another sovereign. Somehow they had thought Victoria would live for ever. The Queen had been ailing for a few days, but no one, at least not in Woodford, thought she would die. Her death stunned them all. They were bereft; the world would be totally different; it was the end of an era.

On 2 February, the day of the Queen's funeral, Hannah closed the Coffee House. She told her family that they had closed it for their father's funeral and they must not do less for the Queen. The girls found black ribbon and made arm bands and Hannah put a broad band of black crepe along the top of the shop window and round the door. A sense of dismay, of fear for the future and dread of change, hung over them all.

But life did not stop with the death of the Queen – 'The Queen is dead, Long live the King', King Edward VII – and of course the family found that the change of sovereign made very little, if any, difference to their mode of life. Everything went on just as before.

Shortly after their father's death, Hannah had purchased two ladies' bicycles for Daisy and Rhoda, which they had quickly learnt to ride, with much laughter and some bruises. Lily also learnt to ride, although her feet were unable to reach the ground and cycling for her was very hazardous along the gravel roads.

These bikes had fixed wheel drive, which meant there would be no respite from pedalling even when going down hill. Free wheels came in a short while later, and a friend of Daisy's from church fixed the bicycles with them. The girls very much enjoyed their cycling expeditions and covered considerable distances even though the roads were stony and the going at times difficult.

In the June of 1901, the annual Meet of Cyclists took place. This Meet had started in 1881, the year Daisy was born. It was an event greatly enjoyed by the locality. The procession started at the Eagle Hotel at Snaresbrook, and by a devious route which included passing through Woodford Green, ended up at the Royal Forest Hotel, Chingford, where the various floats and individual entries were judged.

Rhoda, Daisy, Lily and Aubrey watched on the Woodford Road as the procession went by. The floats, all of which had to be cycled along, were most imaginative and wonderfully executed. One cycling club went as the Yeomen of the Guard, with a strong male chorus; another as H.M.S. Pinafore with a boat propelled by a cyclist. In fact Gilbert and Sullivan were well represented on this occasion. As the procession passed the Green, the Woodford Military Band played stirring music and volunteers with collecting boxes went amongst the crowds gathered to watch, asking for money for the local hospitals.

Daisy said that the Meet got better and better each year but did not think she'd ever dare to dress up and take part in it herself. Aubrey, on the other hand, thought that he would like to. This was the beginning of the heyday of the bicycle. Clubs proliferated. After all there was countryside on London's doorstep. Epping Forest was still covered with a carpet of bluebells in the spring and primroses and violets nestled along the lanes with cowslips growing in the meadows. All these could be seen, enjoyed and, unfortunately, picked in great quantities, without the rush of cars forcing the cyclists into the hedges.

However, London was creeping ever outward gobbling up and destroying the countryside in its way. In the village there was talk of an electric tram service. This was opposed by most of the inhabitants of Woodford Green but favoured by those living in the bordering urban district of Walthamstow. Times were changing. The Queen's death had indeed brought an era to a close.

Daisy and Rhoda could see many things around them that needed improvement. One of these was brought forcefully to their attention one rather cold evening in the autumn. Daisy had decided to make chips for the evening meal. She had put a large pan of fat on the range while preparing the potatoes in the scullery. No one knew what happened next but Rhoda who was reading at the kitchen table suddenly saw the whole pan full of fat catch fire. She gave a loud shriek and Daisy rushed in. For a moment both sisters watched in horror; then Rhoda with great presence of mind, grabbed a large lid and managed to slide it over the flames at the same time moving the pan off the heat. Unfortunately, however, a tea towel hanging over the range to dry caught fire. Aubrey hearing the commotion ran in shouting that he'd get the fireman. Daisy told him they needed water and quickly ran into the scullery emerging with a large jug full. The flames were soon put out and very little damage was done.

When David came home later he noticed the scorch marks on the wall above the range and asked what had happened. He looked serious and remarked that Woodford was not equipped to fight a fire. There was only a hand pump with a leaky hose and in order to obtain this dubious equipment a key had to be obtained from the policeman who was the only person who knew which firemen were on call. By the time the pump could be got to a fire the building would be burnt down.

Hannah remarked that she had been worried about fire for some time and that there had been talk in the village about making better provision for fire-fighting. The nearest proper fire station was in Leytonstone some three miles away.

Just before Christmas, Hannah purchased an upright piano which was proudly installed in the parlour against one of the walls. Her favourite piece of music at the time was 'The Maiden's Prayer' and she offered the grand sum of half-a-crown to the first of her children who learnt to play it. Lily was not interested and Rhoda, although she loved music and helped to teach singing at school, was a very poor pianist. Of course it was Daisy who won the half-crown. She practised that piece until she mastered it and then proudly performed to the rest of the family. She never forgot 'The Maiden's Prayer' and when a nonagenarian, could still play it perfectly.

Unfortunately, however, the piano had been placed right up against one of the walls in the parlour and the parlour walls were discoloured with damp. The dampness penetrated the piano and in a short while many of the notes became unplayable. Hannah and, of course, Daisy, were very distressed. They got in touch with the manufacturers who sent out a craftsman who removed, repaired and replaced the damaged keys until the instrument was nearly back to its original condition. Just one note right at the far end of the bass clef remained silent. The piano was afterwards moved to a position considered suitable by the craftsman and is still, to this day played, albeit not so enthusiastically as when Daisy was alive. In fact Daisy played it nearly every day until she was 97, her favourite music being hymns from the Baptist hymnal.

Daisy was quite proud of her prowess on the piano and she had now become the pianist at the little Mission Hall at the back of the Coffee House which the family attended on Sunday evenings.

Hannah and Alfred had always been nonconformists and Sunday by Sunday had attended the Congregational Church at Woodford. When Ada was old enough they sent her to the Sunday School there. Unfortunately the behaviour of the other children attending shocked her parents. The boys would run out shouting and laughing after being dismissed and push rudely past any parents waiting by the door. Hannah had also heard that the behaviour inside the school was as bad as that outside. Ada's parents wondered what to do and eventually, having heard good reports of the Church of England All Saints' Sunday School, decided to send her there. This was a remarkable decision at a time when the schisms between the various factions

Plate 8 – The School on the Green, c 1933

Plate 9 – Olive and David just married

Plate 10 – Richard, c 1912

Plate 11 – The Coffee House, c 1933

Plate 12 – The Coffee House, 2001

Plate 13 – The Woodford Cycle Meet outside the Congregational Church (by kind permission of Vestry House Museum)

Plate 14 – The Woodford Meet of Cyclists, 7 June 1902

of the Christian Church were very pronounced. Nevertheless Ada's parents spoke to the Vicar who agreed to let her and, later, the other children, attend and said he would not insist that they learn the offending dogmas, such as the catechism and creed. So when the vicar came round to test the children on these, Hannah's offspring would say proudly that they were not allowed to learn them and the vicar, with a little smile, would pass on to question the next child, knowing quite well that the Coffee House children probably knew the catechism and creed better than those being questioned. How could it be otherwise with the others around reciting them regularly each Sunday.

Daisy loved All Saints' Sunday School. Towards the end of her time there her teacher was Miss Fitzpatrick, the daughter of the Vicar. She was always very kind to Daisy and took an interest in her problems. She also went to see Esther and brought her gifts when she was ill.

Every year at Christmas time, the Vicar and his daughter would arrange a party for all the Sunday School children. Daisy and the others looked forward to this event excitedly. It was held on the first Saturday after Christmas in a large room in the Wilfrid Lawson Temperance Hotel near the Castle at Woodford Green.

The room would be gaily decorated so that the children would enter with Oh's and Ah's of delight to find a magnificent spread laid out for them, with a Christmas cracker for each child. Having thoroughly enjoyed their tea the children would all sit quietly for the prize giving. Books were presented to all those who had attended Sunday School regularly throughout the year. After a few games they would finish the evening with a magic lantern show. On one occasion Mr Fitzpatrick had obtained scenes of Equatorial Africa which were shown to the delighted children. There were no cinemas or television with which to compare this entertainment and to those children it was a magical evening.

The Coffee House children were fortunate. Their home was only a few minutes' walk away. Back they would hurry carrying their new prizes. Once in the warm kitchen they would examine their books more closely. One child might be rather disappointed but another delighted and then comparisons would be made with the inevitable 'you're lucky, that's nicer than mine'. However such comments did not mean a great deal for all the children shared the books and the discussion was just a formality.

Sunday evening was the time when the family joined together for a meal and though Lily might get most of the supper ready one of the others would usually prepare something special, maybe a recipe obtained from a friend or, perhaps, read in a magazine. Sometimes these treats were appalling flops. A recipe Daisy had found for 'orange compote' somehow misfired on one occasion. She had prepared this carefully but in the end there wasn't as much as she expected, so being self-sacrificing, she gave the others large helpings, keeping a little back for herself. Unfortunately it turned out to be

57

intolerably bitter. She had left in the pips and pith which should have been removed and the result was unfortunate. Daisy looked eagerly at her family for the praise which usually came for the 'special treats'. The spoons were raised to lips and then put rather hurriedly down. There were odd grimaces on the faces of the others and then David commented that it was rather unusual and no doubt an acquired taste. However, Aubrey, a lot less tactful, just said straight out that it was awful and he could not eat it. Then poor Daisy took a mouthful and was horrified. It was quite uneatable. Such catastrophes were, however, unusual and mostly the special dishes were acceptable and praised fulsomely.

Daisy's life now mainly revolved around church, Coffee House and family and her experience was therefore necessarily somewhat restricted. She rarely went far from home and when she did it was for her annual holiday.

The first time she went on holiday was in the summer following her father's death. Daisy had been looking rather pale and Hannah felt she needed a change. Daisy had a friend named Olive whom she had met at church and the two girls got on well together. Olive was training to be a nurse and her mother also thought her daughter needed a holiday. Where should the girls go? They must go where they would be safe and a Christian Holiday Home was decided on. The one which they finally chose was at Bexhill-on-Sea, and arrangements were made for the girls to stay for a fortnight. Daisy was tremendously excited as this would be her first journey so far from home.

Aunt Susannah had again come to the rescue and agreed to help her niece whilst Daisy was away. One of the neighbours who had a cart offered to take Daisy and her case down to the station and her mother decided to go along to see her daughter safely on her way. They arrived at the station to find Olive already waiting with her mother. The girls just had time to greet each other when their train drew in and the holiday had started. At Liverpool Street Station they changed to the underground railway, arriving in good time at Victoria Station for their train to Bexhill. Daisy found the journey extremely interesting and, having obtained a corner seat sat with her eyes glued to the window, afraid of missing anything. Nevertheless, despite the excitement of the journey, by the time they eventually arrived at Bexhill both girls were tired. They made their way to the Holiday Home and then disappointment rapidly set in.

Olive and Daisy were greeted at the door by a very severe looking woman who told them to follow her. She led them up to a bleak bedroom which contained four beds and the minimum of furniture for four people, together with a washstand with a large chipped china bowl and a large white jug. There was worn brown lino on the floor and a thin rug by each bed. The weather had turned wet and the room looked excessively drab and the view from the window was nondescript. It did not look out to the sea as Daisy had hoped. The woman who had met them at the door was the matron in charge. She seemed rather unpleasant as she looked them up and down. In a rather harsh tone of voice she informed them that supper would be at 6 o'clock and that they must not be late as unpunctuality was not tolerated in the establishment. Lights were to go out at 10 o'clock after which there would be no talking and water for washing could be fetched from the room next to the lavatory. She continued by telling them to read all the rules on the door and that prayers were held every morning at 7.30 a.m. and all guests were expected to attend. After delivering this very chilling introduction the matron left the room.

The two girls looked at each other in dismay. This was not what they had expected. As they had entered the room they noticed signs of occupancy and assumed that the other two guests had already arrived. Whilst they were unpacking the door opened and in came their room mates. They were sisters, the elder one was called Violet and the younger Maude. They were extremely friendly and cheerful. Daisy and Olive expressed their dismay with the place but the other two girls just giggled and said they were determined to enjoy themselves despite that old frump.

After Daisy and Olive had unpacked, all four girls went for a walk along the front. The rain had stopped and flashes of sunlight lit the sea. Daisy was enthralled with all she saw. It was in fact the first time she had seen the sea and it was a wonderful experience. She longed to go down on the beach and explore this new world. The spirits of all the girls rose and in a short while they were chatting happily and making plans for the holiday. Suddenly Maude realised the time and, commenting mischievously that unpunctuality was not tolerated in the establishment, suggested that they hurried back. The others agreed, especially as it would be their first meal at the Holiday Home. Daisy wondered what the food would be like as the walk and the sea air had made her hungry.

When they arrived back at the home they went to their bedroom to tidy themselves and then wandered down to the dining room. This was another drab room with shiny white oilcloth on the tables. Plates of thick slices of bread and margarine were already in place and when all the guests were seated a lengthy grace was said by the Matron. After this a plate with a small piece of boiled cod, unsupported by any form of sauce, was handed to each guest. This together with the bread and margarine was apparently the only supper they were getting, except for a cup of strong tea. After the scanty meal had been eaten a prayer of thanks was piously said by the Matron and the guests were allowed to leave the room.

The four girls went up to their bedroom. Daisy groaned that she was still hungry and it had been a terrible meal. Maude complained that she could not sleep if she was hungry. Olive, the practical one commented that there was plenty of time before 10 o'clock to go out and find some more food. When returning from their walk Violet had noticed a restaurant not far away from the home. It was agreed that they would try there. They had not reckoned on having to spend most of their holiday pocket money on food, but that, in fact, was what happened. The food at the Holiday Home did not improve but the girls became good judges of the little restaurants round about and managed to stave off the pangs of hunger quite satisfactorily.

Halfway through the holiday, the weather turned hot and then for poor Daisy the worst happened, she started her period and, in accordance with the old wives' ruling of the time, could not even paddle. The other three girls tried the joys of sea bathing from a machine, while Daisy sat disconsolately on the promenade. Her friends joined her after half an hour with damp hair and glowing faces. They had obviously enjoyed the experience and were sorry Daisy had missed it.

Despite the rather grim holiday home and the sour-faced matron, despite the fact that most of their money had to be spent on additional food, the girls all enjoyed themselves. They were young, it was a new experience and they got on well together. In fact so much did they enjoy their holiday that they decided to go away in a foursome the following year, if possible, though, of course, to a different place.

Maude, the younger of the two sisters, was a shorthand-typist. She had been trained at Clark's College. This was the first time Daisy had ever met a girl who worked in an office. She had always considered this men's work. Until meeting Maude her ideas of careers for girls of her class had been bounded by schoolteaching, if one was very clever or ambitious, or else working in a shop, dressmaking, millinery or, failing anything else, domestic service. The idea of office work interested her and she regretfully wished that someone had suggested it to her. Now it was too late to change, her mother relied on her, they were working well together and the shop was prospering. Perhaps, thought Daisy, office work might interest Lily when she left school.

Daisy had made lasting friendships on this holiday. Her previous rather tenuous friendship with Olive was strengthened and continued throughout their lives. Daisy was still visiting Olive when the latter was blind and deaf and living in a nursing home in Maldon, Essex, in the 1970s. Maude had died about ten years earlier but until her death had corresponded regularly with Daisy.

8
Fortune and Misfortune

The Carpenter family lived in a cottage near the Coffee House. Mr Carpenter was an artisan who earned on an average £3 a week, which was considered an excellent wage for those times. His wife was a good friend of Hannah's and his daughters Christine and Olive had been schoolmates of Daisy and Rhoda. Christine was attending the pupil teacher centre with Rhoda, but found the work a struggle, and, as she confided to Rhoda, did not really think she wanted to be a teacher. For a long while David had been attracted to Olive, the younger of the two sisters, a gentle, pretty girl. He now began to seek her out on all possible occasions and the friendship between them gradually deepened into love. To the general satisfaction of both families the young couple announced their engagement. Olive's parents approved of David, knowing him to be a serious, hardworking and intelligent young man and Hannah felt that she could not have wished for a better daughter-in-law.

Daisy, however, had watched the friendship grow between her adored brother and Olive with rather different feelings. She had found David gradually change from the confidant and friend she had always loved, to a rather critical acquaintance. The crunch for her came one sad Sunday when they were all going to evening service together. David was waiting impatiently for the others. He had arranged to sit with Olive that evening and Daisy was keeping them all waiting. In fact the day before she had bought a new hat and it took longer than usual to put it on. She could not decide the best angle to wear it. She tried it this way and that and, at last, proud of her appearance she joined the others, expecting compliments. David looked her up and down rather disparagingly and commented on her large feet which were so much more clumsy than Olive's. Poor Daisy had always been aware of her large feet. She turned bright red and had difficulty in holding back tears. Hannah saw her daughter's distress and told David that it was quite unnecessary to criticise Daisy in that way especially as she looked so pretty that evening. The damage, however, was done. Daisy's pleasure in her new hat was completely destroyed and so was a little more of the confidence she had in herself.

David realised that he had hurt his sister and, being basically a very kind young man, immediately tried to make amends. But Daisy would never feel quite the same about him again, recognising, as she had not before, that his allegiance was now elsewhere. From that time her chief friend within the family would always be Rhoda and throughout their lives the sisters always retained a strong affection for each other.

Rhoda's life, however, was expanding. In March 1902, she won a King's Scholarship. Woodford Pupil Teacher Centre had entered four of its students for the award and all four passed. Two obtained first class passes but Rhoda and a friend, another Daisy, gained second class marks. Though Rhoda was very disappointed with her second class classification, the Centre was very pleased with her. Fifty per cent of all the entrants from the other centres had failed so the four from Woodford had really done very well. Later that year 15 pupils from the Centre, 14 women and one man, passed their pupil teacher examinations. That man, Ebenezer Farmer (or Eb as he preferred to be called), some years later married Rhoda.

The Church at Ray Lodge was entering more and more into their lives. The Sunday School there was expanding and needed more teachers. Daisy was asked if she would take a class, and agreed. There was still a sum of £370 owing on the new church building and so efforts were made by all interested to pay off this amount. In the November of that year Ray Lodge Church held a Sunday Schools Scholars' Exhibition in an attempt to raise money. Many local firms had stands showing their work and displaying their products.

David demonstrated an electric battery, which was in fact a toy. Electricity was generated by rapidly turning a handle. Brave people would be asked to hold brass handles and would then get a small electric shock. If people joined hands the current would pass round in a circle. This little machine was later passed on to Daisy's children who also used to be fascinated by, and a little afraid of, it. It was a novelty and at a penny a go raised some money for the funds. There, nearby, was Olive running the flower stall, looking very pretty and, when not selling flowers, gazing at David with adoring eyes. She thought him very clever and that he looked quite the most distinguished young man in the room. Daisy, looking after another stall, wished that she had stayed at the Coffee House instead of her mother. Watching David and Olive made her feel so lonely. She was now 21, not a very great age, but since the unfortunate affair over John Collins, no other man had shown more than a passing interest in her. She did not want to run the Coffee House with her mother for ever. She, who had so passionately wanted to be a teacher, now wanted her own home and her own children just as passionately. She could not imagine meeting anyone suitable.

Over at the other side of the room Richard Hardy was talking to a friend. His eyes kept resting on Daisy. He considered her the most attractive young lady in the room. He would like to get to know her better but did not think she would be interested in him. His family lived in one of the poorer cottages in the Ray Lodge area and he was sure Daisy's family would look down on him. In fact Lily had been in the same class at school as his sister Dora. Dora and Lily had not really liked each other. Lily had considered that Dora had put on airs to which she was not entitled whilst Dora was quite aware that Lily looked down on her.

Early in March 1903, Rhoda learnt that she had passed the Pupil Teachers' Scholarship Examination. This time six students had been entered from the Woodford Centre and all of them had passed. The Superintendent of the Centre was extremely pleased especially as Rhoda and the only man in the class, Eb Farmer, had obtained high places in the first class. Most of the candidates from other centres had obtained third class passes or had failed. Scholars who passed this examination were entitled to enter a teachers' training college.

Rhoda was delighted. For some time it had been her ambition to go to college and at last it was about to be realised. The next hurdle to overcome would be to find a college that would take her. Many of the teachers' training colleges were rather biased against pupil teachers, preferring to take students with more academic training and qualifications. However, Rhoda's high place in the examination would ensure her a greater chance of getting into a good college.

She did not know where to apply and sought advice on all sides. She discussed the matter with Miss Clutton, the head of the girls' section of the Green School. Miss Clutton mentioned the matter to the Governors. The school was proud of Rhoda. She had done very well indeed at the Pupil Teachers' Centre and some of the credit for her achievement came to rest on the school. Miss Spicer, who was a governor of the school, took an interest in the case. She came to see Rhoda and Hannah to discuss the options open to the girl. It was Miss Spicer who suggested that the girl should apply to Homerton College, Cambridge. Homerton was a Congregational Church foundation, as opposed to the more usual Church of England ones, and Rhoda and all her family were members of the Congregational Church.

Rhoda was delighted with the idea and thrilled at the thought of going to Cambridge, even if she was not to be at the University itself. She applied to Homerton and was accepted to start that autumn. The whole of the family at the Coffee House were very proud of her. She would be the first one to go to college and was indeed breaking fresh ground. From this time on Daisy more and more accepted her sister's views and became somewhat afraid of expressing her own opinions. She lost faith in her own judgement, which was a pity because in many ways she was the more practical of the two.

Rhoda collected all the clothes and equipment she would need for college, so much it seemed, and a trunk was purchased so that her possessions could be sent on in advance. It was only when the trunk was corded and labelled, awaiting collection, that Daisy realised she was losing Rhoda. She tried to be cheerful but she was going to be so lonely without her sister, after all she had already lost David, her earlier companion, who now had little time for her.

Rhoda also was feeling rather depressed. Excited and thrilled at the thought of college, she was looking forward with considerable apprehension to her new life. For the first time she would be living away from home, amongst strangers. She might find it difficult to make new friends and she knew she would miss Daisy and her mother.

The evening after Rhoda left for Homerton, Daisy wandered out of the Coffee House and along to the open forest land near her home. The evening was warm and the countryside peaceful, but there was no peace for her. She felt resentful and trapped. She loved her mother dearly but surely there should be more to life than work in the Coffee House. What future would she have? Rhoda had been lucky. Not only had she the excitement of going to college but she also had a great friendship with Eb Farmer, who had also been accepted at a Training College in London. Daisy was quite sure that this friendship would end in marriage, but she, Daisy, had nothing.

When Daisy returned home she was irritable with Aubrey and totally unsympathetic to Lily, who had now left school but not yet decided what to do except that she was not going into service. Daisy was not interested in Lily's prospects. Why should she be when she had no prospects of her own? For a few days she continued in this frame of mind and then her natural cheerfulness gradually reasserted itself. Of course Hannah had noticed her daughter's moodiness and had understood the reason for it. She had, however, no remedy to offer. Daisy must accept her position in life and make the best of it. Nevertheless she encouraged her daughter to take part in the activities of church and mission hall in the hope that she might find an acceptable husband.

Aubrey was now old enough to attend evening service on Sunday, although he would much have preferred to stay at home. One wet and stormy Sunday, Hannah and the family left the shop together. Aubrey had been comfortable by the fire and was rather indignant at being made to go out on such an evening, even if it was only a few yards to the mission hall. He grumbled incessantly, complaining that he knew he had a cold coming and if it was draughty in the hall, as it usually was, he would be unable to go to school next day. Hannah, however, would have none of it telling the lad that Chapel would be good for him and that of course he must go as there was nothing wrong with him.

The service over, the family all returned home, except David who was having supper at Olive's house. They longed for the cosy warmth of the kitchen and the pie keeping hot on the range. When they reached the shop the main door was open. Hannah asked who had been the last to leave. Daisy said that it was her but that she had definitely shut the door. With much trepidation Hannah pushed the door wide open and, groping for the matches, lit the gas lamp. She gazed around her in horror. Drawers had been pulled out and overturned, cupboards emptied, vases upturned. Chaos reigned in the shop and the kitchen was as bad. Needless to say there was no pie keeping hot on the range, just an empty plate and crumbs.

They crept upstairs and the same sad state of things existed there also.

64

Daisy was terribly distressed, all her little valuables had been taken including the locket with Esther's hair in it. The shock of the robbery had numbed them all and it was finally Aubrey who suggested that they send for the police. He was told to get the local policeman by Daisy, who wanted the boy out of the way. Directly he had run off Hannah began to sob. She did not know how she could manage with all her savings stolen. She would not be able to pay the rent. Daisy said she would fetch David and then they would have to see what could be done.

The policeman arrived with Aubrey at the same time as Daisy returned with David. There had been considerable agitation for some time at the inadequacy of the Police Force. The population had grown and was still growing and many people thought there should be definitely more policemen for the area, but as yet nothing had been done.

The policeman looked around and said importantly that he would make a report, but there was really very little help he could give. He did say that it was a good thing the little chap had gone to church with the rest because the villains might otherwise have harmed him. Aubrey turned rather pale but said stoutly that he would have chased them away. Secretly he was glad he had not been left at home. After that horrendous Sunday Hannah noticed that her youngest son no longer wanted to stay at home on his own in the evenings when the family went to church.

Hannah, David, Daisy and Lily, with hindrance or help from Aubrey, gradually got things sorted out and found the extent of their loss. They were not wealthy so the thieves' haul was small but to Hannah and her family it was a tragedy. Small pieces of jewellery the girls had collected over the years were taken. Any cash hidden around the shop had gone and nothing easily disposed of and worth any money at all was spared.

Hannah was in despair but neighbours and friends at the church came to their aid. Money was loaned or given and in a short time things were back to normal. Except, that is, for the feeling that strangers' hands had sorted through their possessions and that for weeks their habits had been studied by hostile eyes. Hannah bought fresh locks for all the doors and at night and whenever the family were out, the place was left as safe and secure as locks and bolts could make it. The thieves, of course were never found.

When the cold weather set in that autumn, Rhoda, away at Homerton, wrote home saying that she could not sleep at nights, she was so cold. Please could her mother somehow send her a quilt? If she could not sleep, she would not be able to work during the day. Hannah, ever concerned for her children's welfare, bought the warmest quilt she could afford and then was faced with a problem. How could she get it to Cambridge? She was puzzling over this when Miss Spicer called. She had continued to be interested in Rhoda and was wondering how she had settled into College life. On being told about the quilt, she immediately offered to take it to Homerton. It would give her an opportunity to see the College and Cambridge. Hannah was delighted and so, of course, was Rhoda. Rhoda was very proud to receive a visit from Miss Spicer. It raised her in the estimation of her peers and she was also very grateful for the quilt. She was now cosy and warm at nights and able to sleep and wake refreshed and enthusiastic for her day's work.

Daisy was delighted when Rhoda came home again at Christmas and for that holiday the sisters were again the close friends they had always been. Daisy loved hearing about Rhoda's college life. How awe-inspiring Miss Allen, the Principal, was. How critical she was of Rhoda's Essex accent, and how hard they were expected to work. However, Rhoda was clearly enjoying the academic life, and though she was not going to excel she would obviously gain her teaching diploma without too much effort. She also talked enthusiastically about the friends she had made, until Daisy began to feel a little jealous. She was, however, delighted to hear that she would probably be able to spend a weekend at the College with Rhoda and meet all the people her sister had talked about.

Eb Farmer, knowing that Rhoda was home on holiday, made a point of meeting her ostensibly to compare notes on their courses. He was, however, very attracted to her and the attraction was mutual. It would, however, be many years before their relationship would be able to proceed beyond friendship.

On Rhoda's return to college, Daisy's depression set in. Again she was irritable with her younger brother and sister for a short while but she had realised, when Rhoda was at home, that she might have found College life and the studying far harder than her more academic sister. Daisy had also become interested in her activities at Ray Lodge and now had many friends there.

In 1904 David married Olive Carpenter. For some while David had worried about his prospects. He had not been progressing as well as he had hoped and thought he might do better if he set up in business on his own. There was much discussion within both families about this and finally it was decided that David should try running a small shop. He borrowed some money and with what he himself had saved, rented a sweet shop in Leytonstone. He and Olive planned to run this between them and they were sure they could make a success of this venture.

They were married in Woodford Congregational Church. David was 24 and Olive about three years younger. They were very much in love. They believed they would make a success of the shop and they did. Sometimes Lily, who had not yet decided what she wanted to do, would help but usually they ran it on their own. They were prepared for hard work and it was hard work, but they were working together, for themselves and for their future which now looked rosy.

Within a year they had paid back their debts and within another year had put enough money aside for David to consider another venture. This time he rented a larger shop at Watford. It was decided that Olive's sister Christine would take over the first shop which would supply her with a good income, with a little of the profit going to the young couple, and, when she wished, Lily could help Christine at Leytonstone.

Alas for dreams. David this time had not done his homework sufficiently well. The shop at Watford was badly placed. It was on the wrong side of the road and, however attractive they made it, however hard they worked, they barely managed to cover expenses. Added to this worry was the fact that, under Christine, the other shop was not prospering. Christine had heard some rumour that the block of little shops in which David's stood was going to be pulled down. She believed this and from that time took very little interest in her work. Business began to fall off and soon David was as worried about that enterprise as he was about the other. Added to these anxieties was the fact that Olive was now pregnant. David, of course, was delighted that he would soon become a father, but was also concerned about the extra expenses in which this would involve him. When she was occupied with the baby he would lose a good deal of his wife's help in the shop.

David carried on as best he could but became more and more worried. His mother and sisters were very perturbed as obviously his health was suffering, but they could not interfere and anyway there was little anyone could do to help. Lily would sometimes help Christine in the Leytonstone shop and sometimes would go over to Watford and help there, but for the most part the young couple had to work out their problems on their own.

The baby, a little girl, was born. David and Olive were very proud of her and named her Christine after her aunt. She was much admired by both families. But David, though now a proud father and very happy in his marriage, became more and more worried. He was getting further into debt and could not see how things were going to work out.

Although it was summer he caught a bad cold. His wife begged him to rest and stay indoors. He could look after the baby whilst she managed in the shop on her own. David, however, was stubborn. He had planned to go over to Leytonstone and try and sort out the muddle there. Olive argued in vain that a day would make no difference to the situation and that he should stay in especially as it was such a cold and wet day. David however refused to take her advice. He set out in the driving rain and arrived at Leytonstone wet and chilled. He could not change his clothes, worked hard all day and by the evening felt really ill. He returned to Watford a very sick man and took to his bed with a high temperature.

Olive was seriously worried. The baby also had a cold and she could not do everything on her own. She wrote to her mother, who arrived two days later to help. David by this time seemed a little better but rather weak. His mother-in-law thought he should go away for a few days and said that they had relatives in Bournemouth who would be glad to have him. She sent them a telegram saying he would be arriving the next day.

David set out for Bournemouth in a very weak state of health. He was running a temperature and had a pain in his chest. It was surprising that he reached his destination at all and it was obvious to his hosts when he arrived that he was a very sick man and they were extremely worried. He went to bed immediately. His breathing was difficult and the pain in his chest very bad. Next day he was worse. A doctor was called who diagnosed pneumonia. David became delirious, calling for Olive and muttering about his business affairs, which were obviously still very much on his mind. In the end he gave up the struggle and died, away from his wife and his own family.

A telegram was sent summoning Olive but David was dead before she could reach Bournemouth. Hannah and Olive's relatives travelled down for the funeral and there, far from home, amongst strangers, David was buried, a young man of only 28.

David and Olive had been married for only four years. It seemed a waste of a life. He had been an intelligent, thoughtful man and a kind and considerate husband. His daughter, Christine, young Christine, as she was called, was still a baby and would never remember her father. It was a terrible tragedy for Olive. The shops had to be given up and Olive returned to live with her parents, remaining with them until they died. Although she was a very attractive woman she never remarried and after her parents died she and her sister Christine brought up young Christine together, and made a very good job of it. They always kept in touch with Daisy and the rest of her family and were much liked by Daisy's children.

Poor Olive did not have an easy life at all. For many years she and her sister were caretakers for a shop in Walthamstow and lived in a flat above the shop. When they retired they went to live in a house in South Woodford. Unfortunately this suffered bomb damage during the war and they were all evacuated to safety. After the war the house was repaired and both sisters returned to it. Young Christine was married when another tragedy struck Olive – she had a stroke which paralysed her right side and deprived her of speech. For seven years she lived a very frustrated existence, looked after by her devoted sister, Christine.

David's life and marriage had really foundered on the result of a medical examination. Had he been accepted by the Post Office, it is reasonable to assume that he would have married Olive, had a secure job and, without the stress of his failing business ventures, might well have lived for many years. It seems unfair that a supposed heart irregularity, probably caused by the stress of trundling a heavy wheelbarrow up a steep hill, should have prevented him obtaining work that would not have required heavy physical labour but only mental resources, with which he was well endowed.

Hannah of course was very distressed, as any other mother would be in such circumstances. She had always been so proud of David. He was such a good looking, intelligent young man. She had the feeling that she might have been able to nurse him back to health. After all she had cared for him when young. She certainly would not have sent him to Bournemouth. If her advice and help had been sought the tragedy might not have happened. These feelings may have resulted in some slight coldness towards Olive's mother for a while, but it did not last. Mrs Carpenter had acted for the best, if perhaps unwisely. Of the remaining members of the Coffee House, Daisy was the one most affected by David's death. He had been her favourite brother and playmate until he turned to Olive. After Daisy married she had an enlarged photograph of her beloved brother on the wall of her home and her son was called David in memory of him.

Hannah had borne eight children of whom two had died in childhood and one in his late twenties, but the five remaining all lived until they were octogenarians, three at least becoming nonagenarians, surely a case of the survival of the fittest.

Of course, in 1904, when David and Olive married, life was for them very rosy. However, for Daisy, things were very different. She was now 23 and unmarried with no career except that of helping her mother in the Coffee House. Life seemed to her to have very little to offer. She could not look into the future and see what would happen. She could not know that of all the sisters she would be the only one whose husband would live to old age. In 1904 she had no husband and no one seemed at all interested in her and she was missing her sister, Rhoda.

Towards the end of her first year at College Rhoda asked permission for Daisy to visit her for a weekend. Permission was graciously granted and to Daisy's great delight she was able to stay with Rhoda at Homerton. She thoroughly enjoyed that weekend. Rhoda met her at Cambridge station and then the two girls made their way to the College which was some way out of town. In fact Daisy saw very little of Cambridge but that did not matter. It was not Cambridge she had come to see. It was Homerton that interested her. She met Rhoda's new friends, among them her College 'mother' and 'sister'. The College 'family' was a system devised to help the first-year students settle in more readily. She was also introduced to one or two of the lecturers they happened to meet, and she explored the College, which to her seemed enormous.

On Sunday morning she attended chapel and there she saw Miss Allen, the awe-inspiring new Principal, for the first time. Daisy was surprised to find her a relatively young woman but she sensed the strength of character and determination that were to help Homerton become one of the foremost training colleges. Before reading the lesson the Principal's eyes roamed over the assembled students and fell on Daisy sitting at Rhoda's side. Daisy felt nervous and blushed. She could not understand why she felt that way but thought that Miss Allen had been summing her up and probably found her wanting.

Shortly after that weekend Rhoda came home for her summer vacation and, as she was able to help her mother in the shop, Daisy could go away with her friends on her annual holiday.

Lily was now the problem in the family. She had, of course, left school but did not know what she wanted to do. For a while she helped round the shop, looking after Aubrey, endeavouring to keep him out of mischief. She was always willing to go over to Leytonstone and assist Olive and David in the shop there, but she would have to get a job sooner or later. She was adamant that she would not go into domestic service, asserting to the shocked Hannah that she would rather kill herself. Still, she had to do something.

Finally, Hannah arranged that Lily should work in a dress shop in Leytonstone as an 'improver'. Lily was clever at making clothes and Hannah hoped that this work, doing any alterations required by customers, might lead to something better. When Lily learnt what her mother had arranged she was appalled. This was not what she wanted out of life and insisted that she would not do it. This time, however, her mother was firm. As Lily had not been able to make up her mind what to do, this would at least be a start.

There were several improvers in the shop and poor Lily was the lowest of them. They were supervised by, to quote Lily, 'A sour old maid who was a dragon'. Maybe Lily, so obviously resenting the work, brought out the worst in the lady but certainly the girl disliked her intensely and the feeling was reciprocated. Unfortunately the lady could make things more unpleasant for Lily than Lily could for her. Consequently all the worst jobs were passed to the rebellious girl, buttons to sew on, skirts to hem, buttonholes to make.

Every evening when she came home she was sullen and nothing Hannah and Daisy could do would cheer her. Aubrey, whom she adored, was the only one who could raise her from her depression. Hannah and Daisy both realised that this state of affairs could not last and one night as Daisy lay in bed thinking of her past holidays, and planning future ones, she remembered Maude and the work she did. If Lily had training she could also be a shorthand-typist and work in an office. She was quite as intelligent as Maude. Daisy determined to speak to her mother about this.

The next morning Daisy broached the subject to her mother, telling her that she had been thinking about Maude who liked her office work tremendously. Surely Lily could do something like that? Hannah had not considered such a solution but said that it was quite obvious that Lily could not continue in her present position as she hated it so much. Perhaps Daisy should write to Maude and ask her advice.

As usual on returning from work Lily moaned about her work and how she was put upon by everyone, especially 'the Dragon' who gave her all the worst jobs. At last Daisy could stand it no longer and without saying anything to her sister went up to the parlour and wrote to Maude explaining the position. She asked her friend to please write back soon as she could not stand Lily's grumbling much longer. Maude did as she was requested and Daisy received a letter by return. Maude explained how she had been on a course for shorthand and typewriting and office routine at Clark's College and suggested that Lily should do the same. The nearest Clark's College was at Forest Gate on the eastern outskirts of London and Maude suggested that Hannah should write to the Principal there for particulars.

The next time Lily started grumbling Daisy countered by asking her whether should would like to work in an office as her friend Maude did. Lily stopped grumbling and stared at her sister unable to believe her ears. How could she work in an office, she knew nothing about the work. Daisy explained that she had written to Maude who had suggested that Lily attend a course at Clark's College. Daisy knew that Lily had always been good at school and was quite sure she would be able to manage the course. Lily thought about it for a while and then said she would like to do it and asked for her mother's support.

Hannah was pleased to see her youngest daughter enthusiastic for once as she had been apathetic for so long. She said that she would write to Clark's College to see what could be arranged but until they knew the position Lily would have to stay in her present job as she would need all the money she could get. Lily 's face fell but on this occasion she did not grumble, at last there seemed to be a glimmer of light on the horizon.

Hannah learnt that if the College accepted her daughter, and they would need to interview her to see if she was suitable, she could either take a full office training course of one year or else a six months' course, mainly in shorthand-typewriting. Hannah decided she could only afford the six months' course for Lily and then a problem arose. Her daughter would need pocket money to pay for the various expenses she would incur and yet Hannah did not feel that, if she paid the fees, she would be able to make Lily an allowance as well.

Rhoda was just finishing at Homerton and was applying for jobs locally in Woodford. After she learned that she had gained her teaching diploma, she was accepted as a teacher at Churchfields School, about 20 minutes' walk from home. She was, of course, delighted. Daisy had written to her sister at Homerton explaining what was being planned for Lily and the problem with regard to pocket money. Rhoda then made a very generous offer, which was typical of her. She was now going to earn a reasonable salary and was prepared to make Lily an allowance out of it. Lily was overjoyed. This would solve all her problems.

Lily went for an interview to the College and was accepted for the six months' course. The journey to Forest Gate from Woodford was rather complicated and so the best way for the girl to travel was by bicycle. Everyday, whatever the weather, she valiantly cycled the four miles to and from the College, and she worked very hard indeed. By the end of the six months she was doing 120 words a minute in shorthand and had a good speed and accuracy in typewriting. In fact her speeds were quite as high as those of students who had taken the full twelve months' course. She was quite popular and made many lasting friends at the College and then, of course, regretfully had to leave and find employment.

At that time the acceptance of women in offices was not so general as at present. Shorthand-typing was still a relatively new career for girls and jobs were quite difficult to find. Lily studied the vacancy pages in the newspapers and wrote for many jobs but with no success and then she had a stroke of luck. On the off-chance she went into a firm and asked if they needed a shorthand-typist. She was very fortunate. They had just that morning put an advertisement in a paper which had not yet been circulated. Lily was interviewed, tested and accepted. She had found her first job and this was important. Once she was a shorthand-typist who could say she had experience, there would be more positions open to her.

Lily proved very capable at the work and her new employers were pleased. Sometimes she came home tired, as the hours were long and sometimes the journey difficult. She no longer complained as she had done previously as she found the work often interesting and knew she could do it and do it well. Hannah was satisfied, another of her girls had found interesting employment.

What of Daisy? Of course Daisy was pleased for Lily, after all she had instigated the whole thing. But again a younger sister had passed her by. Both Rhoda and Lily now had interesting jobs and here she was still at home, still in the Coffee House, with, in her eyes, no interesting prospects. No wonder she was a little jealous and a bit curt at times when Lily chattered on about her doings in the office.

9

Daisy and Richard

The pattern of life had now been set for the next few years. Rhoda was a local schoolteacher finding, perhaps, discipline difficult to maintain in a class of 60 girls but, nevertheless, popular with most of her pupils, and a hard-working member of staff. David, married happily, but finding his business ventures a strain until his unfortunate death in 1908 and Lily, an office worker in London.

Aubrey, now growing to manhood, proved to be intelligent and sociable. Like his father before him, but unlike his elder brother David, he would mix with the customers in the Coffee House, would play chess with them and, when old enough, discuss the various pertinent issues of the time. When he left school he went into a solicitor's office and soon became noticed for his ability. Ada's marriage had proved to be an unhappy one and, secretly, Daisy was glad that she had refused John Collins' proposal many years earlier. By this time her sister already had several living children, having also lost twin boys with the dreaded diphtheria.

Daisy was still her mother's deputy in the home and in the Coffee House. Apart from home and shop her life was bounded by the church and activities associated with it and that church was now Ray Lodge Congregational Chapel. She was a Sunday School teacher there and would play the piano when needed. Her friends were mainly members of that church and her interests there in some measure helped to counter the feelings of inferiority she felt at home with both Rhoda and Lily who were now both settled into, what seemed to Daisy, interesting careers.

Rhoda had continued her friendship with Eb Farmer, the one male student at the Pupil Teacher Centre they had both attended before going on to college. He had also got his diploma. However, his main desire was to study science and he was not particularly interested in teaching others, although he proved to be very competent and popular. Their friendship deepened into something much more and finally, in 1912, Rhoda married and, after a cycling honeymoon, she and Eb settled into a home in Wanstead. Daisy, the older sister, remained at home, unmarried, and her mother could not have managed without her.

However, around 1911, Daisy struck up a friendship with Richard Hardy, who was now an enthusiastic member of the Ray Lodge Church. Richard had been an acquaintance of Daisy's for a long while, but there was a considerable difference in their home backgrounds and a friendship had not developed. He had, however, always been attracted to Daisy, and Daisy was feeling very much in need of a friend now that Rhoda was so much involved with Eb.

Richard's father had followed in the tradition of his father who had been one of the pioneer workers in the coal gas industry and finally become manager of St Albans Gas Works, in the middle years of the nineteenth century.

Richard was the eldest son in a family of six children, four girls and two boys. When he was a young child his father was kind and would often do his best to interest and amuse his children. However as he progressed in his work and became outside foreman at the Woodford Gas Works, he necessarily had to walk long thirsty distances from one job to another. What was more natural than that he should call in at a pub on the way for refreshment and this, eventually, led to a habit of heavy drinking and finally to persistent drunkenness. When Richard was eight or nine years old it was usual for him to see his father drunk and quarrelsome. The young boy used to watch the strain in his mother's face as she waited for her husband to come home from the pub and would wish that he could help and protect her from the violence that so often followed. If he ever made the mistake of trying to stand up for his mother all his father's venom would be turned on him and he knew that this upset his mother even more. Richard grew up hating alcohol. It had destroyed his childhood and embittered his youth. He was determined that, if he ever had a home of his own, it would be a teetotal one.

Because of the unhappiness of his home, he turned for consolation to his church. After all his mother, despite her suffering, was a keen member and he adored his mother. His home experiences had made him a reserved youth who found friendship with his contemporaries difficult and it was finally within the church that he managed to find companionship and this in turn cemented his commitment to the Church.

He had, of course, no qualifications when he went out to work as an errand boy at the age of 13. When he came home from his work at night he would wonder what his father would be like and hope and pray he would not be drunk. It was sheer torture to Richard to see his adored mother ill-treated by her drunken husband. Sometimes his father himself realised the deterioration in his family life and would make a determined effort to overcome his weakness and then for weeks at a time, there would be peace in the home. Then maybe, a long thirsty walk, a jeer from his friends for not joining them, and the resolution would be broken and once again the old pattern of life would be resumed. The young man would come home from work to see his mother's strained white face, as she waited for her husband to come home drunk and quarrelsome. Richard became very perceptive of his mother's feelings and lived her agony with her.

When he was around 20, a change took place in his relationship with his father. Up until then when his father was drunk the lad had kept out of his way as much as possible, for often the man's anger would fall on his son. The change in their relationship came during a period when Richard's father had been drinking heavily and his son had been getting more and more concerned for his mother's health and safety. Along with his concern for her had come a furious anger against his father. On arriving home one evening the young man was greeted at the door by his mother and the look on her face told him just what a state his father was in. Richard decided that he must somehow bring an end to such an intolerable state of affairs. He heard his father swearing in the garden and then growling as he entered the kitchen. Instead of feeling fear, as he had done on previous occasions, he went into the kitchen and told the older man just what he thought of him.

The father's rage was instantaneous and he started to roll up his sleeves for a fight. But Richard was too fast for him and quickly bent down and picked up a heavy poker. At that moment he could have easily killed his father. Suddenly something inside the youth told him to stop. He dropped the poker and held out his hand to his father. The older man seemed completely overwhelmed, his son's act having brought him to his senses, and they shook hands. Sobered, the father went to bed. Had Richard fought his father he might well have killed him, but the young man felt that, in not fighting, he had acted the coward's part. Nevertheless, from that time a change for the better came over his father and gradually home life improved. However, the son always felt he must be his mother's protector and that he should strive to keep the home going for the sake of his brother and sisters. For this reason, for several years, he put away every thought of marriage and a home of his own.

With the improvement in his home conditions, his involvement in the church's activities increased and he joined with his friends in an endeavour to get a boys' club started. They had some slips of paper typed, inviting boys to come on Thursday to a meeting, and these were handed out to the lads on the Sunday before. Thursday came, and Richard and his friends waited hopefully for the boys to come. They waited and waited and not a solitary boy came near. The friends were not to be defeated for they soon realised what had happened. A fair had arrived in the neighbourhood and in no way could a boys' club compete with the excitements of a fair. Well, if the mountain would not come to Mahomet, Mahomet must go to the mountain, so off the friends went to the fair and there in a field they endeavoured to attract the boys by singing loudly to drown the noise of the roundabout. It took considerable courage to do this and maybe the boys admired them for it. At any rate it proved to be the start of the boys' club which was run by Richard and his friends for a year or so.

Richard's involvement with the church led him to the notice of the Spicer sisters and, learning that the young man did not have a settled job, they offered him employment in the Spicer paper firm. He was asked whether he preferred the counting house or warehouse. He unfortunately opted for the warehouse, and, having started work there, realised he had made the wrong decision. He therefore determined to better himself and set out to take courses in paper technology in the hope that perhaps, one day, he would manage to get 'on the road' as a commercial traveller. He worked hard both at the warehouse and then at evening classes. Sometimes whilst studying at home in the small hours of the morning he would fall asleep over his work and his pen would waver blackly, uncontrolled, over the page he had been writing. However, he obtained various diplomas in paper technology, sometimes gaining merits and doing sufficiently well to be noticed by those in authority. Finally, he was promoted from the warehouse to the counting house, an almost unheard of event in those days. Eventually, after much persistence on his part, he finally got 'on the road' but that was also a long hard battle.

When Richard was 29 his father retired on a pension and he and his wife moved to Whitstable in Kent. Thus the way became clear for their son to marry. All this time he had been much involved with church activities and so, of course, had Daisy. One evening, after church, he suggested that he

75

might walk her home. She agreed and they both enjoyed the experience which was repeated week after week.

The friendship was not without its opponents, the chief one being Aubrey, who really thought his sister was too good for Richard. He had learnt something of the young man's background and used it in his arguments against his sister's friendship. Richard's father was a drunkard, surely there was a risk that his son might eventually become one too. Daisy argued hotly against this. Richard had signed the pledge and would never drink alcohol. He would never take one drink, let alone become drunk. But Aubrey implied that Richard might change later. Rhoda was on Richard's side. She understood Daisy's loneliness and encouraged her sister to continue her relationship with Richard, emphasising his good points. She mentioned his devotion to his mother and said that a good son usually made a good husband. Rhoda was shortly to marry and her happiness would be all the greater if she felt Daisy were settled too.

Finally, Richard asked Daisy to marry him. She had been expecting this for some time and had decided to accept. Richard was overjoyed, but Daisy herself was uncertain. Were they really suited? Richard had not stayed at school as long as she had and his manners were a little uncouth and his accent rather broad. She was afraid that as the years went by these 'deficiencies' would annoy her. She started trying to 'improve' him, and Richard not surprisingly resented it. He loved Daisy for herself and she should love him in the same way. They did not enjoy their walks so much. The young man was constantly aware that Daisy was rather ashamed of him and did not like introducing him to her friends. She then asked to break off the engagement, telling Richard that she didn't think they had enough in common and would be happy. Richard's reply was that he knew they would be happy and that he would do his best to care for her. But Daisy was adamant that she did not want to marry him but would like to remain friends. Of course Aubrey was overjoyed that the engagement was officially over.

Daisy now felt lonelier than ever, and turned to Rhoda for advice. She asked her sister whether she had done the right thing as she was really very fond of Richard and missed him when he was not around. Rhoda replied that she liked Richard and that he was a very sincere and reliable man and would make someone a good husband. She however could not make Daisy's mind up for her. She must make her own decision but she should not let Aubrey influence her as it was much nicer for her brother when Daisy was at home pandering to his needs.

Richard, who had never really given up, started walking Daisy home again on Sundays and, after a little while, when the friendship had re-established itself, asked her, for the second time, to marry him. The young lady was still rather unsure, but agreed. Aubrey was extremely annoyed, claiming that Daisy was definitely giving herself to someone inferior. He was rude to Richard saying that Daisy would inherit money from her relative,

Captain Cozens, while Richard would never inherit anything from anyone and would therefore benefit financially from the marriage. Richard was very upset at the suggestion that he was marrying for money. He knew it was just not true and, of course, Aubrey knew it also, but it was one extra weapon to use against Richard.

Aubrey's hostility towards Richard influenced Hannah's attitude towards him and she, too, was adversely affected by his broad speech and rather uncouth manners. Yet she was able to recognise his good points. Daisy so much wanted her mother's support and yet in this instance she did not get it. Maybe Hannah subconsciously feared the changes that would inevitably occur if Richard married her daughter. Despite the hostility which he met from Aubrey and the disapproval of Daisy's mother he continued with his courtship.

Daisy and Richard now took their annual holidays together, staying at Christian holiday homes. One such holiday was spent at Grange-over-Sands, just south of the Lake District. It was the first time Daisy had seen such glorious scenery and she was thrilled. Richard was a nature lover and through his eyes Daisy saw flowers and birds she would not have noticed by herself. Also she began to realise that other young women found him attractive and this enhanced him in her eyes. At least she did not want him to marry anyone else but was still a little doubtful as to whether she really loved him. She realised that Richard would not wait for ever and that he was beginning to be tired of her inability to make a decision on a subject which to him was cut and dried. He loved her and wanted her and he truly believed she loved and wanted him. Gradually Daisy began to look forward to a life with Richard.

There were other very real problems. What would happen to the Coffee House if Daisy married? Richard would not allow his wife to continue working there or anywhere outside her home and Hannah could not continue without her help. Also, where would the newly married couple live? Richard had not saved up much money. He certainly would not be able to buy a house and to rent a whole house in a pleasant area would cost too much. These matters were discussed at great length. Richard was in favour of renting two rooms in someone else's home but Daisy would not consider this. The problems seemed insoluble and then they were suddenly solved.

Ada knew of course that Daisy was engaged to Richard and looking for a home. She herself had recently lost her husband and was desperate for a source of income to support her family. She asked if she could come back to the Coffee House. Hannah had grown used to working with Daisy over the years and now did not want to change her partner. She was also over 60 and very tired. Rather than work with Ada she decided she would retire. If, however, she retired, would Ada be able to manage on her own? Ada was sure she would be able to cope with perhaps some help from her eldest daughter, Gracy. (Ada ran the Coffee House (later the Forest Café) until 1939.)

Finally it was arranged that Hannah would rent a house in Leytonstone, which would be big enough to provide a home for herself and her two youngest children and also let Daisy and Richard have two rooms of their own. Daisy would be able to help her mother during the day. Richard was not as happy with this arrangement as were the others. He knew that Hannah, Lily and Aubrey disapproved of him and yet what else could he do? Daisy would not start married life in two rooms in a stranger's house and he could not afford anything else. So he accepted the inevitable, determined to do well at work so that he would be able to keep Daisy in the way he wanted to, in a home that was really their own.

It was now 1914. Daisy and Richard married on 18 July. The marriage ceremony of course took place at Ray Lodge Congregational Church and afterwards the young couple, though perhaps now not so very young (they were both thirty-three), set out for their honeymoon at Budleigh Salterton in Devon. They caught the train at Paddington Station and took their places in an empty carriage. Just before the train started a young lady got into the compartment. Looking at Daisy and Richard she realised that they had just married. Out of her bag she produced a newspaper which she opened wide, wide enough for Daisy to see the headings. It was the Suffragettes' news sheet, defending the right of women to have the vote and equality with men. Daisy was not a suffragette but when she was determined to get her way she usually did so. Richard was determined to be the one to make the decisions in the family but usually it was Daisy who had the final say. Richard was very much a Victorian in his attitudes towards his wife and family but times had changed even if he did not accept it.

On 28 June 1914 Archduke Francis Ferdinand of Austria and his wife were assassinated by a Bosnian student, starting a train of events that finally plunged the whole of Europe into war. It was the invasion of Belgium which brought England and the British Empire into the war on 4 August, a day or so after Daisy and Richard returned from their honeymoon. It was indeed a terrible time for a young couple to be starting their married life.

Richard did not volunteer as did other members of the family. Aubrey, for instance, joined the Navy as a writer. Richard's brother, Andrew, fought throughout the war in the army. In June 1916 Daisy and Richard became the proud parents of a little girl, Winifred. Because of his wife's pregnancy Richard was able to postpone his call-up for a while. This was the time of the first air raids on London in the First World War and Richard vividly remembered seeing the shooting down of a German Zeppelin that fell to earth at Potters Bar.

Eventually, in December 1916, Richard was called up and, due to defective eyesight, was not sent on active service but acted as an officer's clerk attached to the Royal Army Service Corps.. He was, however, away from his beloved Daisy who was finding life very difficult looking after her mother, Lily and of course baby Winifred. Aubrey was now away in the Navy.

78

Richard would send Daisy as much money as he could from his army pay but they both had a struggle to meet their commitments. Then, whilst he was still in the Army, on 11 November 1918 the armistice was declared and he immediately wrote to his adored Daisy a very descriptive letter of the excitement of that great day.

At 11 a.m. his officer said to him that the war ought to be over by now. He had barely said this when someone raced in with the news and then one whistle was blown and the whole world erupted with sound. Everywhere there was uproar, hooters, whistles, bells sirens all going full blast. A church bell close to Richard had been tolling for the dead, someone had died from the terrible flu raging throughout Europe, when its toll soon changed into ringing victory. When he went into the town he saw soldiers wearing bunting, rags or paper, or anything that looked like a flag, and troops marching along had little flags in their helmets. Guns or anything that could hold a flag was draped with one. The shops were closed, the pubs were raided and the churches wide open. He ended his letter with the final remark that there had never been such an hour in human history.

The war had taken its toll of the family. Mainly from the effects of the deadly influenza virus that had devastated the weakened soldiers and civilians. Daisy caught it but did recover, although it took a long time. Andrew, Richard's brother, had gone all through the war but caught the 'flu' and instead of going into hospital tried to get home. He died on the way. Ada's eldest daughter, Grace Collins, was a driver in the Royal Air Force and she also caught the 'flu', contracted pneumonia and died just after the end of the war.

The terrible war had ended and true married life for Richard and Daisy was about to begin. The Coffee House, which had started a new life with the Collins family, went on prospering until the Second World War.

Epilogue

It is interesting, nearly 90 years later, to see how the lives of the main actors in this story evolved. Fate can almost be seen to have played a part. The two sisters with careers both lost their husbands at relatively young ages. Eb Farmer died when he was in his thirties, after only nine years of married life, during which he and Rhoda had one son, aged only five at the time of his father's death. From then on she was forced to return to teaching in order to keep herself and her child.

Lily lost her husband later, when he was in his fifties, after a long and

79

tragic illness. She too returned to work where she remained until entitled to a pension. She also had one son but he had reached manhood, indeed was doing his National Service, at the time of his father's death.

Daisy, who had no further training after schooldays had finished, whose life had been circumscribed by home and family and who would have found it more difficult to earn a living to keep her three children, never had to. She was the only one of the sisters whose husband lived to old age. Richard died when he was 79. So the sister who felt that she would have no future was the one whose future became the most secure.

Daisy and Richard, our mother and father, never had a great deal of money and during the time of the depression when trade was bad, Richard, then a commercial traveller for Spicers, did not sell enough goods to cover his income and became in debt to the Company. He had to work very hard to pay off a portion of this sum, the rest being remitted. Unlike representatives today, he did not have a firm's car and the customers he called on were small printers and stationers scattered over East London. He would buy a shilling all-day tram ticket and endeavour to make as many calls as he possibly could. When he realised how badly he was doing he set himself an almost impossible agenda each week. But he won through and finally paid off his debt and began to earn good commission. In 1936 he was called in to see the Sales Director who told him that the firm had watched his sales gradually but continuously rise and on the strength of this he was given a new area and a company car. He was by then 55 years of age and had to learn to drive and pass his driving test, which he did the second time round.

An ironic final twist to the story comes from the fact that Richard *did* inherit money. His sister, Dora, had gone out penniless to Canada willing to take any work that came her way, even scrubbing floors. In the event she started in the Hudson's Bay Company and ended up as ladies' ready-to-wear buyer for the company in Calgary. She died undergoing surgery for tuberculosis in the Mayo Clinic in the United States. She never married and the money she had saved was passed on to her sisters and brother and to their children. It was not a fortune but was just as much as Daisy's share from Captain Cozens.

By the end of his life, Daisy's family had come to like and appreciate Richard for his kindness and willingness to help them in time of trouble. Those who earlier had decried him, later spoke of him only with affection.

This story, however, really ends at the end of the First World War, a war that greatly changed society. Our mother, Daisy, used to say that the world was quite a different place from the one she knew as a child. Both wars accelerated the difference. We cannot perhaps say the same because, though life was very different in our childhood, the origins of it as we know it today were already there: cars, aeroplanes, electricity, telephones, and the clothes we wore when young would not look out of place today. It is, perhaps only in the final decades of the twentieth century that our generation has seen the great changes wrought by microchip technology with computers, the world-wide web and e-mailing.

However, our mother's childhood and life up to the time she married seemed to her and to us to belong to another world and therefore we have left the story in that world and not brought it into ours.

The Coffee House Movement

In Victorian times many of the working and labouring classes lived lives of great poverty and deprivation. One of the few places available to them for relaxation was the public-house, where amidst companionship and with cheap alcohol, despair and the struggle for existence could be, for a short while, forgotten. But drunkenness could lead to violence and drunken or semi-drunken men could be roused to frenzy by agitators, especially as bitterness and unrest were often very near the surface. Consequently the public-house was frowned on by the upper and middle classes. Nevertheless some of them realised that working men needed a place of retreat, a place where games could be played and cheap food obtained in a relaxed atmosphere away from the stresses and discomforts of home.

This concern with drunkenness and dislike of the public-house led to a rather remarkable Coffee Tavern Movement. This movement sprung up all over the country starting around the 1830s and carrying on until the First World War. The movement was certainly associated with the churches in some areas. Occasionally a nonconformist church and an Anglican church joined together to start such a project. For instance in 1861 at Streatham Common the Vestry and the Congregational Church raised subscriptions to buy the freehold of an old public-house which was rebuilt and turned into a Temperance Coffee and Working Men's Lodging House. This was a large affair containing a reading room, seven small bedrooms and a concert and lecture room for 500 people. But this was one of the more ambitious projects. Many were small houses, centrally placed, where there would be sufficient space for games to be played – dominoes, draughts or chess – and where good cheap food would be served.

The movement was country-wide and by 1881 it was reported, for instance, that in London there were 300 such houses and in Liverpool 41.

The coffee houses had their own newspaper, which was started in 1837, named the *Coffee Public House News* and it continued under this title for several years until it became the *Temperance Caterer*. From this newspaper it is possible to get some idea of the movement and the scale of its activities.

Women were not generally catered for. They did not, it was believed, need this type of entertainment, indeed they would not have time for it if they looked after their homes and children properly. But in some areas Women's Coffee Houses were started. In Poplar in 1900 a Miss Philimore had erected, at her own expense, a building which comprised a home for working-class women with a Coffee House downstairs. She must also have been quite broadminded for the times, because she had incorporated a large room for dancing when this was considered sinful by many churchgoers. Also, in 1878, a coffee tavern called Princess House was opened in Brompton Road for women only, who could stay there for 3s 6d and 4s 6d a week.

Normally, however, the coffee houses were for the use of men only. Boys were discouraged as when they were allowed in they were often noisy and interfered with the men's games. As the boys could not use the coffee houses, the obvious places for them to go to meet their friends were the public-houses. But this was what the coffee house movement had wished to discourage. Therefore, if the boys were to be encouraged away from the pubs they had to be catered for somewhere else. For this purpose boys' rooms were opened in some of the coffee houses. In Sheringham on the East Coast for instance, at the Two Lifeboats Coffee House, there were a classroom, a boys' room and also stabling for horses. There was a coffee house opened for boys in Kensington, too, but the local vicar said that they required very strict supervision.

Companies were set up to promote the coffee taverns and these offered £1 shares to the public. One such company was the Bradford Coffee Tavern Co which paid a 10 per cent dividend. It claimed that its coffee houses and taverns catered for all types of persons, luxurious coffee houses or temperance hotels for the well-to-do, while, for those with less money, there were houses with billiard rooms and, for the poorer working men, taverns. Public-houses were often converted, sometimes the old name was retained and sometimes a completely new one given. In some areas houses were purpose-built and, in others, suitable shops or buildings were converted as for example in Tenby, where the Coffee House had originally been a draper's shop.

That the movement was supported by the upper class is made very clear. In West Clandon, Surrey, Lord Onslow changed a pub into a village club and coffee house for the men on his estate. On one occasion the Earl of Derby, supporting the movement, said in a speech that one acre of good land cost £60 which equalled 3d per square yard. How much better it would be, therefore, if instead of paying 3d for a glass of beer the men put it towards buying land. What the men would have done with the land or how they would in fact buy it was not made clear.

In the earlier years covered by the *Coffee Public House News* it is clear that it was difficult to obtain good managers but, by 1881, in the 'vacancies' and 'jobs wanted' columns, the seekers after manager's jobs well outnumbered the jobs vacant. Later, criticism was made of the quality of the food and tea served and organisations were advised not to take managers on recommendation only but to examine credentials carefully and interview applicants.

In Northern England the term 'Cocoa Tavern' would seem to have been widely used to denote the same type of institution. There was for example a Nags Head Cocoa House in Chester and, in Liverpool, the British Workmen's Cocoa Rooms which served no food, only soft drinks. The men frequenting this house apparently preferred to bring their own food.

The houses were open for very long hours in order to compete with the public-houses. The Douglas Cocoa Rooms in Fetter Lane, London, were still open at 2 a.m. A check on who frequented the rooms at that hour found them to be full of compositors, printers, van men and packers from the newspapers – and also law writers. Two well-spoken but very poorly dressed men proved to be 'down and out' barristers.

Whether the movement did have an effect on drunkenness it is difficult to say. It probably did cater for a need, that of supplying reasonably priced food to working men, and the prices were reasonable. For instance, a plate of roast beef cost 5d, steak and kidney pie 7d, meat and potato pie 5d and steak pudding 5d, potatoes were a penny a helping. As well as this, however, in 1887, when the movement was perhaps at its strongest, it was claimed that there was a falling-off of excise duty, which might suggest that less alcohol was being drunk.

Although it was largely a movement designed by the upper and middle classes to discourage drunkenness and the risk of revolt in the lower orders, in some instances the coffee houses were used by philanthropically motivated people for alleviating hardship. For example the Cross Keys Coffee Tavern in Roberts Street, Chelsea, supplied breakfast in batches to large numbers of children daily. The tavern was not big enough to accommodate them all so they were given their meal in a local hall and, additionally, food tickets were issued to people living in the area who were in deprived circumstances.

However, whatever the reasons for the movement, it was, as can be seen, widespread. Apart from the food at reasonable prices the houses were expected to offer warmth – a large fire – non-alcoholic drink, amusements ranging from draughts and chess to billiards and, in some cases, music hall entertainment. This latter died out quickly as it was impossible to afford the better acts. There were coffee houses or cocoa taverns in places as far apart as Festiniog in Wales, where there was a purpose-built house, to Sheringham on the East Coast, and Poole in Dorset, where the house was built by the owner of a pottery for his workpeople. The houses were in towns or in the country, wherever it was thought there might be a need. For example, in Southall, Middlesex, which in 1880 was still a country district, the vicar would arrange for coffee barrows to be taken from the coffee house to the men in the brickfields. The movement was still in existence at the outbreak of the First World War but thereafter seems to have disappeared. With changing times the needs had changed. Cheap restaurants like the Lyons Tea Shops in London had opened in many areas.

As will have been seen in the preceding story, our grandparents ran one of these coffee houses and, in a very different guise, the building is still there in Woodford Green behind the Castle. It was while we were trying to find out how our grandparents originally became involved with this that we realised that our particular coffee house was not one on its own, but part of a large country-wide movement. Why or how our grandparents had been chosen to run the Coffee House, when Hannah had been taught fine needlework and Alfred had been a carpenter, our mother, Daisy, never knew. However, many years later it came to light that, while Hannah was in service in a big house in the area, she became pregnant by Alfred. Her employers (who are presumed to have been the Spicer family because that family took such a continuing interest in Hannah's family), thought so much of Hannah that they set the couple up in the Coffee House on their marriage.

The preceding tale is about that coffee house and the family that lived in it at the beginning of the twentieth century, according to stories told to us by our mother and her sister, and incidents recorded in the local newspapers.

Loughton and District Historical Society Publications List

Transactions No 1 (1970)*: ISBN 9028 9300 9, £1

Transactions No 2 (1974): ISBN 9028 9300 7, £1

Pohl, D J: *Loughton 1851 – the Village and its People* (1988)*: ISBN 9028 9302 5 £3

Elliott, B: *History of the Loughton and Chigwell Police* (1991): ISBN 9028 9303 3, £2

Russell, V J and E H Dare]: *A Walk Round Chigwell* (1992), 75p

Pond, C C: *A Walk Round Loughton* (2002), £1.25

Ambrose, P: *Reminiscences of a Loughton Life* (1995)" ISBN 0952 53440 1, £5.25

Paar, H W: *Loughton's First Railway Station* (1996)*: ISBN 0952 88050 4, £3.50

Hunter, R, Elliot W H and Pond, C C: *The Life of Robert Hunter 1823-1897, Lexicographer, Missionary, Geologist and Naturalist* (1997): ISBN 0952 88051 2, £5

Pond, C C: *History of the Loughton Methodist Church and of Methodist Expansion in SW Essex* (1998): ISBN 0952 88052 0, £4

Whiting, A: *The Loughton Roding Estate, From Cattle-Grazing to Double-Glazing* (1998): ISBN 0952 88053 9, £3

Wilkinson, D: *From Mean Streets to Epping Forest: The Shaftesbury Retreat, Loughton* (2000): ISBN 0952 88054 7, £3

Waller, W C [C C Pond, ed.]: *Notes on Loughton 1890-95* (2001): ISBN 0952 88056 3, £1.50

Morris, R S: *William Chapman Waller 1850-1917: Loughton's Historian* (2001): ISBN 0952 88055 5, £7.50

Morris, R S and Pond, C C (eds): *Loughton a Hundred Years Ago* (2001): ISBN 0952 88057 1, £5.50

Waller, W C [R S Morris, ed.]: *Notes on Loughton – II: 1896-1914* (2002): ISBN 0952 88059 8, £2.00

Lockington, E and Trickey, W: *The Coffee House at Woodford* (2002): ISBN 0954 234 1 4

[The society was previously known as the Chigwell Local History Society and the Chigwell and Loughton History Society]

All books are softbound (except *William Chapman Waller 1850–1917*, which is hardbound). Titles marked * are out-of-print, or only a few copies are left in stock. Items can be had by post (cash with order – cheques payable to Loughton and District Historical Society) from Forest Villa, Staples Rd, Loughton, Essex, IG10 1HP at the prices given – post free in the UK, cash with order. For post abroad, with payment in dollars or other currencies, please write or e-mail (Loughton_Ponds@hotmail.com) first. Overseas postage charged at cost.

10 per cent discount on direct sales to schools, libraries and record offices. Books sent on invoice after official order. Books are also available at similar prices to personal callers at the Loughton Book Shop, 150 High Road, Loughton